Home Office Research Study 214

Evaluation of the Youth Court Demonstration Project

Charlotte Allen, Iain Crow and Michael Cavadino
Centre for Criminological and Legal Research
The University of Sheffield

Research, Development and Statistics Directorate
Home Office

Home Office Research Studies

The Home Office Research Studies are reports on research undertaken by or on behalf of the Home Office. They cover the range of subjects for which the Home Secretary has responsibility. Titles in the series are listed at the back of this report (copies are available from the address on the back cover). Other publications produced by the Research, Development and Statistics Directorate include Research Findings, the Research Bulletin, Statistical Bulletins and Statistical Papers.

The Research, Development and Statistics Directorate

RDS is part of the Home Office. The Home Office's purpose is to build a safe, just and tolerant society in which the rights and responsibilities of individuals, families and communities are properly balanced and the protection and security of the public are maintained.

RDS is also a part of the Government Statistical Service (GSS). One of the GSS aims is to inform Parliament and the citizen about the state of the nation and provide a window on the work and performance of government, allowing the impact of government policies and actions to be assessed.

Therefore -

Research Development and Statistics Directorate exists to improve policy making, decision taking and practice in support of the Home Office purpose and aims, to provide the public and Parliament with information necessary for informed debate and to publish information for future use.

"The views expressed in this report are those of the authors, not necessarily those of the Home Office (nor do they reflect Government policy)."

First published 2000
Application for reproduction should be made to the Communications and Development Unit, Room 201, Home Office, 50 Queen Anne's Gate, London SW1H 9AT.

Foreword

In November 1997, the Government's White Paper 'No more excuses: A new approach to tackling youth crime in England and Wales' set out plans to reform the youth justice system. Legislation in the Crime and Disorder Act (1998) and the Youth Justice and Criminal Evidence Act (1999) took many of the proposals forward, which are currently undergoing evaluation. However, as a more immediate response to proposals in the White Paper, the Youth Court Demonstration Project was conceived as an attempt to change the culture of the Youth Court.

The Youth Court has been shown to elicit the least public confidence. Reform, therefore, seemed necessary. This current research into the Youth Court Demonstration Project has investigated ways in which the culture of the Court might change, independently of any legislative or structural change. Some of the changes were successful, some less so, but the overall feeling from both pilot areas is that the project was beneficial, and that lessons can be taken to other courts.

David Moxon

Acknowledgements

We wish to express our gratitude to all those at the courts involved in this project for the time and help they have given in making this research possible. We are especially appreciative of the practical assistance of the court clerks and their staff, who have responded so patiently to the intrusions into their daily work.

We also wish to thank members of the Home Office and the Lord Chancellor's Department for their support, and would especially like to mention Claire Flood-Page and Siobhan Campbell for the work they did in preparing newsletters for the courts.

Charlotte Allen
Iain Crow
Michael Cavadino

Contents

* *Further appendices giving detailed results of the questionnaires
completed by court personal can be obtained by request from:
Dr. Siobhan Campbell, Home Office RDS CCJU,
Room 824, 50 Queen Anne's Gate, London SW1H 9AT.*

Aims and implementation of the Demonstration Project

The aims of the Youth Court Demonstration Project were to provide:

- a Youth Court which is more open and which commands the confidence of victims and the public

- processes which engage young offenders and their parents and focus on the nature of their offending behaviour and how to change it

- a stronger emphasis on using sentencing to prevent future offending.

The Demonstration Project took place in two areas; one consisting of a single court located in the centre of a medium-sized town (Rotherham), and the other (Leicestershire) a county with five courts. One of the Leicestershire courts was sited in the city centre, and the rest in the surrounding county.

It was found that, in general, the aims of the project were successfully communicated to those involved, although the third aim of using sentencing to prevent future offending was not seen to have such a high priority as the other two.

Despite some reservations, there was broad agreement with the aims of the project on the part of the majority of those involved. The aims were addressed by a series of initiatives in each of the areas designed to:

- increase engagement with offenders and their parents

- experiment with different court layouts

- encourage attendance by victims and the press, including the lifting of reporting restrictions in certain cases

- provide feedback to sentencers about sentencing and other aspects of the courts' work.

The project was implemented in a broadly similar manner in both areas, although there were some differences, both in the emphasis placed on different aspects of the project, and in the times when different initiatives were introduced. Both areas arranged training events in connection with the project, the main purpose of which was to give magistrates the opportunity to develop their communication skills so as to engage with defendants and parents more effectively. Magistrates who took part said that the training gave them more confidence in engaging with defendants.

Engaging with defendants and their parents

It was felt by all concerned that, prior to the project, the defendant had been a largely passive observer of what happened in court. Although some magistrates had talked directly to defendants before the project started, most did not. The project had the effect of bringing the young offender into proceedings more, so that (s)he realised that what was happening in court was because of what (s)he had done.

Magistrates were advised that although they may take some part in proceedings prior to a finding of guilt, such as explaining who is in court and what is happening, any significant engagement with defendants should only take place after a finding of guilt. Consequently most engagement took place during sentencing hearings.

Magistrates' increased engagement with defendants and their families was regarded as one of the most welcome and successful aspects of the project, and did not appear to increase the length of time taken to deal with cases. This is probably because magistrates asked some questions where previously they may have asked none, rather than because there was a significant increase overall in the amount of dialogue taking place.

Although the project showed that a greater degree of engagement could be successfully achieved, if the developments initiated by the project are to be encouraged to take place more widely, then more training and more guidance regarding good practice is needed.

It should also be noted that there were other elements of the initiative that could inhibit productive engagement with young offenders, such as the presence of victims and the possibility of the offender being named, and a careful balance needs to be struck between achieving different and sometimes conflicting aims in the Youth Court.

Changes to the court environment

A number of changes were made to the layout of the Youth Court, which included changes to where participants sat in relation to one another, and the magistrates sitting in the well of the court rather than on a raised platform. In addition, defendants and others taking part in proceedings were asked to remain seated, except to be identified at the start of proceedings and to be given decisions. Other changes included ensuring that defendants and others knew who the various people in the court were and explaining what was happening more, and these were generally well received.

Because of the existing architecture, the ability to make changes to court layout was sometimes restricted, and the flexibility to vary court arrangements is something that may need to be considered when commissioning new court buildings.

There were mixed reactions on the part of court personnel and defendants to the changes in layout that were made. Some felt that, despite initial reservations, it was possible to get used to the new arrangements and that they facilitated greater engagement. Others felt that space became very restricted, with people sitting uncomfortably close to one another. There was also some initial concern that the dignity of court proceedings might be impaired, but after a while this became less of a concern. Fears that the changes might lead to security problems also appear to have been unfounded.

Some changes were regarded as having worked better than others. For example, having defendants' parents sitting next to, rather than behind, their children was regarded as an improvement, whereas sitting in the well of the court was less popular with some magistrates.

If the practice of magistrates sitting in the well of the court were to be adopted more widely, then consideration may need to be given to removing the existing raised platform in order to make the best use of the available space, or at least making it easier to change between layouts by having a low raised movable platform rather than a fixed bench. The indications from a follow-up study were that those involved became more used to the new arrangements with the passage of time, and this aspect of the project was regarded as having had the biggest impact on the culture of the Youth Court.

Attendance by victims

There was considerable support for the principle that the victims of crimes should be able to attend Youth Court hearings, and efforts were made in both areas to encourage victim attendance. However, there were also practical concerns. These included:

- whether the defendant could be identified to the victim

- making sure that victims got the right information about when hearings were taking place

- the possibility that having spent some time waiting for a case to be called, little might happen that would be of interest to the victim at a particular hearing, and the victim may need to make repeated efforts to attend

- ensuring that the victims were looked after by someone, and told if for some reason a case was delayed

- that they should have somewhere to wait where they would not be in contact with defendants

- that there should be adequate space for them in court away from the defendant

- that they may need to be asked to leave at certain points in the proceedings

- that they may attempt to interject in proceedings and be resentful if not allowed to

- that they may have unrealistic expectations that would lead to disillusionment with the process.

It was also felt by magistrates, staff and defendants that the presence of a victim could inhibit productive engagement with the offender, although it is not clear to what extent this did in fact happen because so few victims attended. There were indications that most victims did not particularly want to attend court, and few did during the project, except as witnesses. What seemed to be most important to victims was knowing about the outcome of a case. If victims are to feel able to attend the Youth Court then some effort will be needed on the part of the court, both to make victims aware that they can do so, and to ensure that adequate provision is made for them. The police also have an important role to play in informing victims about cases and their outcome.

Attendance by the press

Prior to the start of the project the press rarely, if ever, attended Youth Court hearings, and it was felt that they were only interested in the occasional sensational case.

One of the courts initiated discussions with their local newspaper, and arrangements were made for a journalist to attend the court on a regular basis for a trial period. This resulted in an increase in the reporting of Youth Court cases, as well as a number of more general articles about youth justice. It was felt that this had been a productive and worthwhile exercise, and could result in the public becoming better informed about youth justice and the Youth Court.

However, care needs to be taken to ensure that an increase in reporting does not in itself lead to a public perception of, and concern about, an increase in crime. There were also indications that the presence of the press might inhibit productive engagement between magistrates and young offenders and their families. It is difficult for a local newspaper to maintain a journalist at court on a regular basis, and regular press attendance did not continue much beyond the trial period. The experience of the court where the initiative took place suggested that courts need to be proactive with regards to the media, to make regular efforts to inform the press about what is happening, and to encourage more contact between Youth Courts and the local media.

Lifting reporting restrictions

The fact that defendants cannot normally be named was one factor putting the press off covering the Youth Court. Reporting restrictions had not been lifted at either court prior to the start of the project.

Although it was felt that it was useful for magistrates to have the power to lift reporting restrictions on occasions, there was broad agreement that this was a power that would be used only occasionally, in instances where the public needed to know that someone was a serious and persistent menace. There was concern that naming a young offender could be counterproductive and give the young person involved an enhanced and undesirable status amongst his or her peers. Magistrates also felt that there was little point in lifting reporting restrictions if the press were not present.

During the course of the project restrictions were lifted once at each court and were reported in the local press. There needs to be a clearly understood procedure by which the press can apply for the lifting of reporting restrictions.

Feedback to sentencers

Although magistrates' courts produce information about their activities, in the past this has tended to focus on administrative and procedural matters such as workload and time intervals in dealing with cases. Before the project started relatively few details were available about such matters as court sentencing patterns, breaches and reconviction rates, although the Youth Justice manager in Rotherham had produced information at Youth Court User Group meetings about the sentences imposed by the court.

During the course of the project discussions took place about the type of feedback that magistrates might like to have regarding youth justice matters at their court and, in conjunction with the Home Office Research, Development and Statistics Directorate, newsletters were produced and discussed at subsequent meetings. This development was welcomed by magistrates and other court users, who were particularly interested in receiving information about reconviction rates and the extent to which sentences are breached or completed.

Despite the popularity of such information, it was noted that care is needed in interpreting the data, particularly reconviction rates, since a variety of factors can influence such a measure. It was also recognised that the value of such information tends to increase with time, as it becomes possible to consider developing trends.

There is a cost attached to producing such information. If the task of producing feedback to the court is to be undertaken on a regular basis then there has to be an agreement about how it is to be done, who is responsible for compiling the information locally (probably Youth Offending Teams in future), and appropriate provision has to be made for the work needed to produce the results. Asked how those involved would like to receive such information, there was a preference for it to be produced quarterly, and to be made available in the form of a newsletter, which could then be discussed in an appropriate forum.

Impact of the project

In response to a questionnaire circulated in mid-1999, some nine months into the project, there were mixed views regarding its impact, with half of those who responded saying that they thought it had had little impact. But asked the same question nine months later, in February 2000, the proportion saying they thought there had been little impact had shrunk to not much more than a third, and more than half of those expressing an opinion thought the impact had been beneficial, suggesting that the changes had taken some time to make themselves felt. The follow-up period seems to have been a time when it was possible for those involved to adjust to the changes as part of their daily manner of working.

Although the project was not seen as particularly concerned with changing the way the Youth Court sentenced people, some magistrates said that engaging in discussions with offenders had on occasions caused them to reconsider the sentence they were initially inclined to impose, and in one of the areas involved there was a significant shift in sentencing patterns.

The changes introduced by the project do not appear to have had significant financial implications; the only additional costs being the need for training sessions and the production of feedback information.

The changes to the Youth Court introduced by the project do, however, need to be seen in the context of other developments. First, they need to be seen in relation to other changes to youth justice, such as those introduced by the Crime and Disorder Act 1998 and the Youth Justice and Criminal Evidence Act 1999. Second, they need to be seen in relation to human rights developments. Of particular relevance has been the consequences of a European Court of Human Rights ruling, the effects of which appear likely to underline the need to make further progress towards the kind of initiatives introduced by the Youth Court Demonstration Project.

Introduction

Although the Youth Court has many similarities with the adult magistrates' court, there are also important differences. On the one hand the Youth Court has a formal environment, with the magistrates usually sitting on a raised bench apart from the rest of the court. However, unlike the adult court the Youth Court sits in private (Children and Young Persons Act 1933, s. 47) and there are restrictions on reporting (CYPA 1933, s. 49). The Youth Court operates with a Panel of magistrates who receive special training, who are under a duty to have regard to the child's welfare (CYPA 1933, s. 44). Courts do have some discretion about the way they work, and practice varies in England and Wales. But on the whole the result of a system that is like the adult court, while at the same time different from it, produces a setting that attempts to balance judicial requirements with a regard for the age and limited experience of those who appear in court. In particular, for those not familiar with the Youth Court, there can be a lack of awareness about exactly how it works and what ends it is seeking to achieve. The Home Secretary, Jack Straw, likened this lack of awareness of the work of the Youth Court to a "secret garden".[1] The importance of the public being aware of the work of the Youth Court has been shown in a recent Home Office Research Study (Mattinson and Mirrlees-Black, 2000). It found that in the 1998 British Crime Survey the public rated the Youth Court worse than any other part of the criminal justice system examined, and that those with the least knowledge about youth crime had the least confidence in the Youth Court. The authors suggested that improving knowledge about youth crime should increase confidence in the work of the Youth Court.

However, research has done relatively little to open up this "secret garden". Although youth crime and young offenders have attracted much attention, and given rise to a considerable literature devoted to explaining their occurrence and what should be done about them, much less has been written about the Youth Court itself. Furthermore, such research as exists is not particularly recent. One has to go back to studies by Morris and Giller (1977) and Anderson (1978) for research that involved interviews with parents and offenders who had appeared in what was then the juvenile court. Even older is the research by Scott (1958) and Voelcker (1960) that looks at the perceptions that parents and offenders have about the youth court and the people working in it. More recent work on the experience of receiving juvenile justice is that by Parker, Casburn and Turnbull (1981). A study by Erickson (1982)

---

1   Speech to the Labour Party Conference, 2 October 1997.

has looked at children's experiences of the Scottish juvenile justice system, and Asquith (1983) provides quantitative and qualitative material about the topics that were discussed in court, and the contribution that parents have made to juvenile justice in Scotland compared with England.

There have been several developments in recent years directed at changing the way that young people are dealt with by the criminal justice system. One of the most notable is the Crime and Disorder Act 1998, which introduced important changes to the way that young offenders are dealt with. In addition to changing the way that young offenders are dealt with following conviction and sentence, the Government also expressed its intention of making changes to the Youth Court itself. However, before introducing any changes on a national basis it was considered advisable to try out some reforms to existing procedure in two areas to evaluate their impact. Consequently, in the summer of 1998 courts around the country were invited to apply to take part in a Demonstration Project. Two areas were selected, and the project started in October 1998, accompanied by an evaluation which is reported here.

Aims and objectives of the project

The specific context for the Youth Court Demonstration Project can be found in the White Paper, *No More Excuses*. Chapter 9, 'Reform of the Youth Court', Para. 9.2 says that:

> '*All too often inadequate attention is given to changing offending behaviour. ... The purpose of the youth court must change from simply deciding guilt or innocence and then issuing a sentence. In most cases an offence should trigger a wider enquiry into the circumstances and nature of the offending behaviour, leading to action to change that behaviour*'.

The White Paper then goes on to say that reform of the Youth Court is needed to provide:

- a system which is more open and which commands the confidence of victims and the public

- processes which engage young offenders and their parents and focus on the nature of their offending behaviour and how to change it

- a stronger emphasis on using sentencing to prevent future offending.

These constituted the three designated aims of the Demonstration Project implemented in two court areas. Rotherham consisted of one Youth Court, while Leicestershire had five individual

Youth Courts. A further description of the areas and the way in which the project was implemented in them is given in the next chapter.

In June 1998 a joint Home Office/Lord Chancellor's Department Circular, *Opening Up Youth Court Proceedings* referred to:

- allowing victims to attend Youth Court proceedings

- allowing the public to attend Youth Court proceedings

- allowing the press to attend Youth Court hearings

- lifting reporting restrictions in the Youth Court following conviction.

Although the circular was sent to all courts, those involved in the Demonstration Project had the role of testing possible useful approaches. Consequently, the Demonstration Project's aims were pursued by addressing specific objectives directed at:

- encouraging magistrates to talk directly to offenders and their parents – "engaging with defendants". Associated with this was the provision of training to develop communication skills

- changing the layout of the Youth Court

- increasing the extent to which magistrates received feedback about court decision making

- encouraging attendance by victims, the press and other interested parties

- facilitating the lifting of reporting restrictions, which normally forbid the naming of under-age defendants, in order to "name and shame" certain defendants.

In a letter to the Chairmen of all Youth Panels in England and Wales, 28 September 1998, headed Improving Youth Justice, the Lord Chancellor, Lord Irvine said:

'The purpose of the Demonstration Projects is to assess what is sensible and practical, and to provide the basis for wider advice'.

It was further explained to those involved in the Demonstration Project that the intention was to try things out, and be prepared to find that some things worked better than others. It is also worth noting that during the time the Demonstration Project was taking place, a number of other developments in youth justice were in progress or envisaged. These included action to speed up the progress of cases in the Youth Court, and the implementation of the Crime and Disorder Act 1998. Of particular relevance were the provisions in this Act to replace Youth Justice Teams, usually composed of local authority social workers and probation officers, with multi-disciplinary Youth Offending Teams, which occurred nationally by April 2000. Also in prospect was the introduction of further legislation in the form of the Youth Justice and Criminal Evidence Act 1999. These other developments are referred to again in the concluding chapter of this report.

The research

The research was carried out in two phases. Following some preliminary visits in September 1998, the first phase started in October 1998 and went on until the end of September 1999. The second phase involved a follow-up period some six months after the first phase, which lasted from mid-February to the end of March 2000.

The research included:

- attendance at key meetings

- interviews with key personnel (including senior magistrates, clerks to the justices, lawyers, and social workers) at the start of the project, towards the end of the first phase, and during the follow-up period

- observations in court throughout the twelve months of the first phase, and during the follow-up period

- a small number of detailed case studies (twenty in each court area), which included interviews with the parties to each case, to examine in more detail how the project affected individual cases. Throughout this report references to the case studies are based on 39 of the 40 cases. This is because one case study involved an offender in Leicestershire who was named in the local newspaper, which was especially relevant to a consideration of the lifting of reporting restrictions. This case is reported separately

- questionnaires to all personnel involved with the Youth Court towards the end of the first phase, and during the follow-up period.

In addition, following a proposal by magistrates themselves, 'logbooks' were kept in the Youth Court where magistrates and other court users could write comments about the arrangements and proceedings, and these logbooks were made available to the researchers.

Finally, a telephone survey was carried out of courts elsewhere in the country where related developments had occurred or were being considered, to find out whether any of their experiences were relevant to the Demonstration Project.

It is worth noting at this point that the research was neither intended nor designed to examine the impact of any changes on reconviction rates amongst those young offenders passing through the courts during the project. Consequently we are unable to make any judgement about how effective the project has been in relation to the aim of reducing offending by young people.

The report covers the main initiatives undertaken as part of the project in each area. In Chapter 2 the court areas and the way they went about implementing the project are described. The developments in other areas are also briefly reported. Chapter 3 reports the results of attempts to encourage magistrates to engage more with young offenders and their families, and Chapter 4 looks at the changes that were made in the layout of the Youth Court. Chapter 5 examines the potential for opening up the Youth Court to victims and the public (mainly as represented by the press and the lifting of reporting restrictions), and in Chapter 6 the provision of information to sentencers about court proceedings and decisions is discussed. Other aspects of the project, including its impact on sentencing and the financial implications of the measures taken, are considered in Chapter 7. Chapter 8 discusses other developments taking place in relation to youth justice which have implications for the work of the Youth Court, and Chapter 9 considers what conclusions may be drawn from the project.

2   Implementation of the project

The two court areas that took part in the Demonstration Project differed in several respects, and approached the project in different ways. Rotherham chose to focus initially on training magistrates to communicate directly with defendants, and because the count was located in a single town was able to consult people fairly quickly in order to act on this. Rotherham's Youth Court also encouraged magistrates to start engaging with defendants as soon as the project started. In Leicestershire a longer period was needed to consult all the benches in the county. Arrangements for training sessions and changes in court layout were deferred until all magistrates had been consulted. Because Leicestershire had several courts, however, it was also possible for some courts to concentrate more on some aspects of the initiative (such as arrangements involving the press and victims), while other courts developed other aspects.

Both court areas produced protocols to guide magistrates and court staff on the issues being piloted in the Demonstration Project. In Rotherham this was produced in November 1998. Leicester City Court's protocol came into effect in March 1999, as did that used by the Loughborough and Melton Mowbray courts. Courts in Market Bosworth and Ashby de la Zouch ratified their protocols in October 1999. The protocols are included in Appendix D.

Rotherham

Rotherham Youth Court operated at a single location. It had 34 Youth Court Panel magistrates, and although two courtrooms were available, there was usually only one operating at a time. The Youth Court normally sat twice a week, but could also sit on other days to hear trials. In this area the main decisions about implementing the Demonstration Project were made by a Steering Group whose membership included the Clerk to the Justices, the clerk with special responsibility for the Youth Court, the Chairman and Deputy Chairman of the Youth Court Panel and the local Youth Justice manager.

The project was discussed in Youth Court Panel and Youth Court User Group meetings throughout its duration. The main decisions were made in Steering Group meetings and developments went to Panel and User Group meetings for discussion and amendment. However, an initial session at the project launch meeting produced the basis for the court's protocol. Acquainting all concerned with the aims of the Demonstration Project and the protocol were the main subjects of meetings in the latter part of 1998. At the start of 1999 training sessions for the magistrates and the sentencing newsletters were discussed in several meetings. Later in 1999, meetings discussed issues raised by the project, especially the new court layout and its effect on witnesses and the press.

In November 1998 the Youth Court Panel approved a strategy in which the initial emphasis of the project would be on engaging with defendants, with training taking place in December 1998. At first it was proposed that training would involve Chairmen and Deputies only, but non-chairing magistrates (commonly referred to as 'wingers') were keen not to be left out, and a second session was arranged for January 1999. However, even before the training was conducted or the protocol produced, magistrates undertook to engage more with defendants by explaining to them who was present in the courtroom and asking questions directly. The protocol subsequently gave guidance on the practice of engagement. In particular the protocol advised magistrates that significant discussion with the defendant should only take place *after* an offender had been found guilty, and to make sure that defence solicitors had the opportunity to have the last word. The Youth Court Panel quickly accepted the practice of engaging with defendants, particularly in sentencing hearings. The stipendiary magistrate especially used more exchanges with defendants as a way of increasing the information s/he received on cases, and on most occasions after January 1999 spoke to defendants and their parents or other supporters before the defence solicitor addressed the court.

For the training on engaging with defendants that took place in December 1998 and January 1999 the court worked with the local Youth Justice team to plan and deliver the training sessions. The training concentrated on acquiring questioning and listening skills through role-play and discussion in small groups. Magistrates were not given 'suitable questions' that they should ask defendants, but were encouraged to use listening skills as a trigger to prompt questions. One feature of the training sessions was the involvement of local young people, who came and joined in role-play and discussion with the magistrates. Their participation was increased for the second training day, which included a mock hearing in a courtroom as an introduction to the issue of changing the layout of the courtroom after positive comments from magistrates in the first session. The young people also subsequently accompanied the magistrates to London to take part in a Home Office/LCD seminar.

Nine out of ten magistrates in Rotherham attended the training sessions, and those attending were asked to complete questionnaires immediately after each session. Eighty-seven per cent of those taking part in the December session thought that the objectives and structure of the session had been acceptable or very good, with another seven per cent thinking they were excellent. Of those involved in the January session, which included more focused work with young people and included role-playing in a courtroom, 67 per cent felt the session had been acceptable or very good, while the other 33 per cent thought it had been excellent. The overall response from magistrates attending both sessions was that the training made them feel more confident about engaging with young people. However, asked to identify further training needs, a common request was for more advice on questioning defendants. In response to a questionnaire sent to all those involved with the Demonstration Project some months later, just over half the magistrates in Rotherham said that they had found the training quite helpful in carrying out their role as a magistrate, and a further third said that they had found it very helpful.

The other main development related to the Demonstration Project in Rotherham was the production of a newsletter giving details of court decisions, which is considered further in a later chapter.

Leicestershire

Leicestershire contained five Youth Courts spread around the county. Throughout the county there were 129 magistrates on the Youth Court Panel, with some sitting on more than one bench. In Leicester City Court the Youth Court sat twice a week in three courtrooms at the start of the project, but shortly after the project started this changed to three days a week in two courtrooms, a change which was not a result of the Demonstration Project. Market Bosworth Court had one Youth Court sitting one day a week, and Loughborough Court had up to three courtrooms sitting once a week. Courts in Ashby de la Zouch and Melton Mowbray had one Youth Court that sat every first and third Wednesday of the month.

The initial meeting that launched the Demonstration Project set up a project Board composed of the Chairmen of the Youth Court Panels and Justices' Clerks from throughout the county to make the main decisions about the project and consult with the county benches. In addition, working groups were set up at each court location in the county. However, the only significant difference between the courts in the county in the way in which the project was implemented occurred in relation to changes in the layout of the courts.

The first project Board meeting identified engagement with offenders and court layout as the issues that should be dealt with as soon as possible, with individual benches implementing their own changes. It was decided that there should be consultation with Victim Support and Youth Justice before anything could be done about involving victims more and feeding back information about court proceedings to sentencers. Youth Court Panel and User Group meetings also discussed the progress of the Demonstration Project, and smaller working groups were set up to draft protocols and recommend new layouts. In early 1999 protocols were taken to Panel and User Group meetings to be agreed, and the project Board meeting in January 1999 discussed producing a sentencing newsletter with the help of the Home Office, and encouraging the press to attend the Youth Court. These issues were discussed further at subsequent project Board meetings, along with plans from Victim Support and the police to increase victim confidence in the Youth Court.

Training for the project was provided at county level, and took place for Chairmen across the county in two training sessions in January and March 1999. These training days concentrated on the aims and skills of engagement, and included discussion of the aims of the project as a whole. As in Rotherham, magistrates were encouraged to develop listening and questioning skills, rather than being presented with a set of example questions. The protocols that were developed further clarified when and how engagement with offenders should occur.

Sixty-five per cent of magistrates in Leicestershire took part in training sessions. This is a smaller proportion than in Rotherham, but is accounted for by the fact that only Chairmen and Deputy Chairmen were involved in the sessions. As in Rotherham, magistrates were asked to fill in a questionnaire about the training sessions in January and March. Eighty-five per cent of those who took part in the January session felt the training had definitely achieved its objectives, but only a third of those that attended the March training session thought it had. Asked how useful they thought the training had been for future application in court, nine out of ten (91%) of those attending the January session felt the training would be valuable for future application, whereas only four out of ten people (39%) attending in March felt that it was. Both training days were exactly the same, so the difference between the January and the March responses may be due to the fact that the project had been part of court practice for longer in March, so the training did not seem as relevant. In response to a later questionnaire sent out during the summer of 1999 some six out of ten magistrates said that they thought the training had been quite helpful to them in carrying out their function in court, and a quarter said that they had found the training very helpful. These proportions were similar to the responses to the same question asked of magistrates in Rotherham, which further suggests that it was the timing of the training sessions rather than their content which resulted in the difference in responses to the questionnaire handed out straight after the training sessions.

In addition to the changes in court layout, Leicester City Court, being the largest bench of magistrates, took the lead in encouraging victims to attend court and in making arrangements with the local press for a journalist to attend court for a time during the project. Further details of these initiatives are presented in later chapters.

Developments at other courts

Before considering in more detail what happened at the Youth Courts involved in the Demonstration Project, it is worth mentioning that consideration had also been given to making changes in the way in which the Youth Court operated in some other court areas around the country. In May 1999 ten other court areas believed to be introducing changes of their own were contacted by telephone and representatives of the courts, usually the clerk responsible for the Youth Court, were interviewed.

The most common actions taken by these court areas concerned magistrates engaging with defendants. In six of the areas this was specifically encouraged. Two of the six areas said that this had always been the case and there had been no recent changes introduced as a result of Government initiatives. In the other four of the six areas magistrates had received specific encouragement to engage since the 1997 White Paper and 1998 circular. In two more of the ten areas there had been some discussions about changes to practice, but nothing had yet been implemented, and in the remaining two there had been no developments.

Two of the ten court areas had experimented with altered layouts, whilst a third said that it already had all participants sitting at the same level in one courtroom, and had recently brought forward the seats for parents in another.

Only one area had taken steps to enable victims to attend court, and this had run into problems concerning obtaining victims' names and addresses so that they could be informed of the timing of sentencing hearings. An attempt had been made to agree a protocol with the police to ensure that victims could be informed, but agreement had proved impossible. Attempts were currently being made to use the CPS instead. In other areas, attitudes varied. At some there was a growing feeling that victims had the right to be involved, but this had not led to any practical initiatives. At others the feeling still prevailed that the Youth Court was not a suitable environment for victims. In all court areas, victims rarely attended except as witnesses.

Press attendance was very rare at all courts. There had only been one occasion in recent years in all ten areas where reporting restrictions had been lifted; this concerned a persistent offender who had made national headlines. No court had made any other attempt to open up the Youth Court to members of the public.

Two courts (both in large cities) had arrangements for sentencers to receive extensive feedback on a wide range of topics concerning court proceedings and decisions. Two others received a certain amount of information on matters such as sentencing and community orders, and in the other six there was little or no feedback to sentencers.

Verifying the aims of the project

Although the aims of a project may be set out formally in documents, it is nonetheless important to ascertain how those concerned with translating these aims into practice perceive them. Interviews with court personnel and court users at the start of the Demonstration Project attempted to capture their views regarding the aims of the project before it was implemented in full. The aims most commonly identified were to involve defendants and their parents more in the court process, to develop engagement with the young person, and to make the process more informal and user friendly. Further comments also focused on communicating effectively with the defendant, including confronting them with what they had done and making them understand the seriousness of the case. Magistrates also mentioned reducing youth crime, sentencing more successfully, treating defendants more fairly, and making sure that they understood the court process. Magistrates in Leicestershire, in particular, hoped that they would be seen in a different light, and that there would be more openness between the agencies in court. Another aim referred to was making the layout of the court more informal or user-friendly. Making the court process more open to the public was discussed by a variety of the interviewees, and improving feedback to sentencers was linked with the aim of improving sentencing.

A questionnaire was distributed to all those involved in working in the Youth Court during the summer of 1999 in which respondents were asked how well informed they felt about the project, what statements they felt best reflected the aims of the project, and the extent to which they agreed with the aims of the project as they saw them. Of all respondents to the questionnaire, over a third (36%) said that they knew a lot about the project and felt well informed about it, with another third saying they thought they knew quite a lot about it. Twenty-two per cent said they knew something about the project, and only eight per cent that they knew little or nothing about the project. It should be noted, however, that the respondents included people who appeared in the Youth Court infrequently, such as social workers and police officers, who may not have received as much information as full-time court staff. Also, some magistrates sit less frequently than others. Looking just at the magistrates who answered the questionnaire, the proportion who felt well informed about the project was much greater than when all the respondents were taken together: more than half the magistrates (54%) said they knew a lot about the project, and more than one in three (37%) said that they knew quite a lot about it. No magistrates said they knew nothing about it, and only nine per cent that they did not know very much about it. There were no significant differences between the two areas in the responses to this question, and it may be concluded that at least the project made an impact to the extent that most people were well aware of its existence, and felt that they knew what it was about.

Respondents were next presented with a series of statements about the project and asked to say to what extent these statements reflected the aims of the project, rating the statements from one ('not at all') to three ('quite a lot'). When the mean scores for each statement were compared, this produced a ranking indicating which statements, in the eyes of respondents, best reflected the aims of the project. The scores and the ranking are shown in Table 2.1 below, for all respondents and for magistrates only.

Table 2.1: Aims of the Demonstration Project

	All respondents		Magistrates only	
	mean score	ranking	mean score	ranking
To reduce the formality of the Youth Court	2.71	1	2.82	1
To encourage magistrates to talk to offenders more	2.67	2	2.79	3
To make the Youth Court more open	2.62	3	2.81	2
To encourage offenders to talk more	2.58	4	2.72	4
To increase public confidence in the Youth Court	2.21	5	2.42	5
To reduce reoffending	2.12	6	2.39	6
To enable the court to arrive at more appropriate sentences	1.83	7	1.90	7
To change the way young offenders are sentenced	1.70	8	1.79	8

Thus, the statements most closely associated with the aims of the project in peoples' minds were 'To reduce the formality of the Youth Court', and 'To encourage magistrates to talk to offenders more'.

Respondents were also asked to what extent they agreed with the aims of the project, as they saw them. The overwhelming majority of respondents agreed with the aims of the project to some extent. Half of all respondents (50%), and more than half of magistrates (57%) said they agreed with the aims of the project a lot or quite a lot, and about four out of ten respondents (43% of all occupations and 39% of magistrates) said they agreed with the aims of the project as they saw them to a limited extent. A very small number of people, 17 in all, including four magistrates (representing 7% of all respondents and 3% of magistrates) said they did not agree with the aims at all.

3   Engaging with offenders and their families

Participants' views

As reported in Chapter 1, encouraging magistrates to talk more with defendants and defendants to respond was rated as an important aim of the project. In initial interviews with key personnel, engaging with defendants was felt to be a good idea, and this was the part of the project that interviewees were most enthusiastic about. Interviewees believed that the main advantage of engaging with young offenders would be that it would lead to the offender realising that *they* had committed the crime that was being discussed in court. It was felt that in the past young offenders had been largely passive, that they had become removed from the court process, and had not confronted their offending behaviour because they were not required to make any contribution to the hearing. In general magistrates had not been encouraged to engage with defendants in the past, and many had felt that it was inappropriate for magistrates to intervene. However, practices did vary, with some magistrates saying that on their own initiative they did speak to defendants. At some of the courts in Leicestershire, in particular, it was already practice for magistrates to talk directly to defendants, and these courts saw this aspect of the project as building on existing practice. Some magistrates intended to increase the extent to which they communicated directly with offenders as soon as the project started, while others preferred to wait until after the training sessions. Several interviewees said that stipendiary magistrates were more likely to talk directly to defendants than were lay magistrates.

During interviews that took place towards the end of the first phase of the research, increasing engagement was one of the parts of the project identified by interviewees as having had the most effect on the court, defendants and their own jobs. It was also the part of the project that most interviewees felt should be retained. Engagement was almost universally seen as having been beneficial for the courts. Magistrates felt that it had had a positive effect on their work, that they felt they were getting to the bottom of cases more, and that the extra information was helping them come to more appropriate sentencing decisions. One magistrate summed up the views of his colleagues when he said:

> "it has enabled you, in the short time available, to make a better assessment of the defendant that you are dealing with, and gain more insight into the problems they may or may not have."

Members of other agencies were impressed by magistrates' increased engagement, and said that magistrates had made an effort to appear more human, to use more accessible language and explain their decisions more clearly, and now appeared to be genuinely concerned with defendants and their welfare. One defence solicitor said that magistrates seemed to be thinking more, whilst another stated that her clients had said things to the magistrates that they had never said to her. However, there was concern that questions could be banal, and that engagement could just be a "pal act" which did not elicit information relevant to the offence. It was also felt that some magistrates were not asking relevant questions or were not responding to what defendants said but were asking questions for the sake of it. One Youth Justice worker in Leicestershire said that he was concerned that the language did not fit in with the eventual sentence. He said that it was hard for the court to be frank and friendly one minute and then send a young person to a Young Offender Institution the next.

At all courts there was an acknowledgement that increased engagement was making defendants and their families more involved in the court case. One magistrate at Rotherham stated:

"It's a change from the defendants sitting back and leaving it to the advocate: it's not an easy ride."

Engagement was seen to make the defendant more aware that their actions had led to the court proceedings. One prosecuting lawyer said it was an improvement to hear what defendants had to say. He said:

"Defence solicitors speak in well oiled grooves and it is refreshing to hear from defendants; you are hearing something new rather than the standard mitigation."

Even though most respondents felt that the engagement had had a positive effect on defendants, this did not mean they felt that defendants were getting an easy ride in court. Having to talk was described as "daunting", "very uncomfortable for a lot of them" and as "being in the spotlight."

As well as the effect on offenders and magistrates, other court staff noted how increased engagement had affected their jobs. Clerks commented that they had had to ensure magistrates did not ask inappropriate questions, and some thought that it might have led to cases lasting longer. Defence solicitors in Rotherham felt that their roles had changed as a result of increased engagement. One said her role had diminished in pre-sentence report and sentencing hearings. Another said that he now tried to pre-empt the magistrates' questions in mitigation. Some Youth Justice workers said that increased engagement had resulted in them giving the court more information, either in the courtroom itself or, bearing in mind what the magistrates might ask in court, in pre-sentence reports.

The logbooks in which magistrates and others wrote comments on individual cases also showed that there was overwhelming approval for the attempt to engage defendants and parents. The practice was seen as positive, beneficial and successful. On two occasions magistrates reported altering an intended sentence as a result. On one of these occasions, the three magistrates sitting (in Rotherham during the follow-up period) wrote:

> "After reading the report, we were not going to tolerate more of the same, and considered custody the only option. After deep discussion with the defendant, we were persuaded that she had changed direction and gave her a probation order to give her an opportunity to prove herself".

The few negative comments concentrated on the extra time that the engaging process was felt to take up, which might cause delays in getting through cases.

In response to the questionnaire sent out during the summer of 1999, there was an overwhelming perception on the part of respondents that magistrates talked more with defendants and their parents since the initiation of the Demonstration Project. Overall eight out of every ten respondents said that magistrates now talked more to defendants and their parents than previously. However, there was a significant difference between the two court areas. In Rotherham, 91 per cent of all occupations and 100 per cent of magistrates said they thought magistrates talked more, whereas in Leicestershire the proportion was only 78 per cent of all occupations and 79 per cent of magistrates. This could be because, as noted above, some of the courts in Leicestershire reported that there was some direct communication between magistrates and defendants prior to the project. Respondents were also asked whether they thought defendants now participated in court proceedings more compared with before the project started. Overall a majority of respondents (51% of all occupations and 56% of magistrates) thought that they did, but again there was a significant difference between Rotherham and Leicestershire. In Rotherham, 71 per cent of all occupations and 76 per cent of magistrates said they thought that defendants now participated more, whereas in Leicestershire only 43 per cent of all occupations and 50 per cent of magistrates thought this.

One of the stated aims of the project was to engage, not only with defendants, but also with parents in order to focus on their children's offending behaviour. But being able to engage with someone depends on them being present, and a frequent concern of magistrates and other court personnel has been the difficulty in getting the parents or guardians of young defendants to attend court. Respondents were therefore asked whether they thought attendance by parents or guardians had changed since the Demonstration Project started. A substantial majority of respondents thought that it had not, with seven out of ten respondents (whether magistrates or others) saying they thought that parental attendance had remained unchanged since the start of the project. This is an area of concern for courts that might need to be further addressed.

When a follow-up questionnaire was distributed to those who worked in the Youth Court in February 2000 most respondents felt that young offenders now participated more in court proceedings compared with before the project started (three-quarters in Rotherham, and over half in Leicestershire). Interestingly, as many as a third in both areas also thought there had been an increase in participation by young offenders during the six months between the end of the initial evaluation and the follow-up period. A high proportion of respondents (seven out of ten in both areas) felt that since the inception of the Demonstration Project magistrates talked more with defendants and their parents or other supporters. More than half in each area (omitting 'can't says') thought that there had been an increase in the six months prior to the follow-up period. A substantial majority of respondents to the follow-up questionnaire in both areas felt that the changes in communication between magistrates, defendants and their families which had taken place had been beneficial, with at least six out of every ten respondents in both areas expressing this view.

Despite such positive responses to engagement in both areas, in Rotherham some concern was expressed at the quality and purpose of engagement by the magistrates in a User Group Meeting in November 1999. As a result a discussion took place between magistrates and members of the Youth Justice Team at the Youth Court Panel meeting that month, and an engagement protocol was produced and distributed to all magistrates in December 1999. This included a number of questions that magistrates could use in engaging with defendants. A feeling was expressed in interviews during the follow-up period that the magistrates' questions had improved as a consequence. A court clerk in Rotherham said his colleagues had been getting frustrated with magistrates merely chatting with defendants rather than addressing offending behaviour, or getting young people to accept responsibility for what they had done. A Youth Justice worker in Rotherham also felt that the protocol had been useful because before it the "magistrates tended to flounder a bit at times". In the court observations that took place during the follow-up period it was noticeable that magistrates were particularly likely to ask offenders about the example that they were setting their younger siblings, and how they thought their offending behaviour could be stopped. It was also noted that magistrates were likely to ask parents what action they had taken in response to their children's offending.

Not everyone approved of the developments in engagement, however, or of all aspects of them. During the follow-up interviews two people in Rotherham (a social worker and a defence solicitor) thought that a couple of magistrates had used engagement as an opportunity to "hector kids in court". The defence solicitor did not feel it was right for a magistrate to speak to the defendant before his or her solicitor, as this could threaten mitigation. Others with reservations included a Youth Justice worker who was concerned that the engagement was benefiting more articulate defendants, and a probation officer who said that magistrates needed more training because they sometimes used technical words or language that young people might not understand.

Despite such reservations, all but one of the interviewees felt engagement had become part of the every day running of the Youth Court. A magistrate in Leicestershire felt that because of increased engagement "the sentencing process is more offender orientated". A stipendiary magistrate believed that it was necessary to be careful about engagement though. He said that if he was thinking of sending someone into custody he spoke to the solicitor rather than the defendant first, and might not speak to the defendant until the sentence because he would not want the defendant to feel that they had been given custody because they had said the wrong thing. A court clerk in Leicestershire and a social worker in Rotherham felt that parents had welcomed the chance to have their say in court, and that engagement had helped in decisions as to whether to bind over parents. In relation to the offenders themselves, a youth justice worker from Rotherham said defendants now told her that they did not feel as if the court was going over their heads quite so much; it was nerve-wracking but they were taking in what the magistrates said and were remembering it. She also noted that her colleagues had felt more confident about going to court and being able to speak to the magistrates, and that the magistrates seemed to be asking their opinion more. A prosecutor in Leicestershire said that it was easier for advocates to give information about young people because magistrates were more willing to be given this sort of information. These comments suggest that engagement has helped the exchange of information between all parties in court.

Views of engagement from the case studies

In interviews with the offenders and their families involved in 39 case studies, ten parents and 12 defendants said they liked the fact that magistrates had asked them questions. Defendants appeared to appreciate having their voice heard in court. One said:

> "At least they know that it's coming from you, and not something that the solicitor's made up."

Parents also relished the chance to speak to magistrates:

"Rather than just sitting there, just taking everything in and passing sentence – it's as if they're taking time to get to know people."

Another commented:

"It shows me that they're not condemning me, they're actually asking my opinion ... asked me whether he's controllable, which I think is a fantastic question, 'cos only the parents would know that".

This indicates that the magistrates gained respect from the parents through the process of engagement.

While the majority of offenders said that they were not worried by the magistrates' questions or found them 'okay', three said that they had worried them. This was primarily because they were worried about giving magistrates the 'wrong' answer and receiving a harsher penalty as a result. Five defendants said that they would have preferred to let their solicitor speak for them and seven said that they had found some of the questions hard to answer. Three said that they thought some of the questions were too personal. One defendant could not understand the fact that the magistrates asked him questions after they had retired:

"It's a bit late isn't it? Asking me what I'd got to say after they'd already decided what they gonna do."

One in six of the offenders and three out of every ten of their supporters said that they would have liked the chance to say more to the magistrates. One defendant said:

"Yes, I would have liked to have said that when I got into trouble for [the offence] it was when I were on drugs – heroin. But I got caught for it months after; it's just something that's caught up with me from when I were on drugs, and I'm not now, know what I mean? That's all I wanted to say but I daren't."

This was one of the defendants who said that she was worried about giving magistrates the 'wrong answer' and suggests that more nervous defendants still need more encouragement to engage with magistrates.

The case studies also presented an opportunity to find out whether engagement had any effect on the magistrates' sentences. Not surprisingly magistrates said that the seriousness of the offence had influenced their decision most, but that engagement with offenders and their family had played a part. In 30 per cent of cases where parents or family were present, their statements were said by magistrates to have had an effect on sentence. In 18 per cent of cases magistrates said that the statement of the defendant themselves had affected the sentence.

Four sets of magistrates did not speak to the defendant in the case study cases. In two cases this was because of a full presentation from the solicitor, and in another because the magistrates had sat at the defendant's trial and had spoken to him on that occasion. The majority (57%) of the magistrates who spoke to defendants said that it had been a useful exercise. One of the magistrates said:

"I'm beginning to feel that it is something that we should have been doing in the past".

The most frequent comment made by magistrates was that engagement had enabled them to discover the defendant and his family's attitude, and had given them a clearer idea of the offence. Magistrates often had positive reactions to what the defendant said:

"He didn't seem to be trying to say things that he thought would impress us. He was just giving us a straightforward honest response."

However magistrates did say that if defendants did not talk this would not prejudice them:

"All you can expect them to do is say sorry, and if they say nothing it wouldn't make me 'up-it'."

Just over a third (37%) of magistrates involved in the case studies said that the defendant had not given them much information, or that the information they received had not been useful. However, some said that the parents' information in the same case had been useful. Only one set of magistrates felt that the questioning had been a negative exercise. This was because what was said in mitigation of the defendant could have led to him having to change his plea to not guilty. One set of magistrates felt that they had delved too far with their questions, because they had found out that the defendant had been in court before, something that the CPS had not been aware of. Other magistrates did recognise that there was a limit to the questions they should ask. One said:

"Part of us might have wanted to know what the devil [the defendant] was doing with that much to drink, but you have to ask what purpose that would serve."

Towards the end of the project a number of magistrates said that the task of engaging was being made more arduous because defence solicitors were starting to pre-empt their questions. One said:

> "It makes it very difficult to ask relevant questions, so in a way, you're finding out more about the person as a rule than you are necessarily about the offence. I'm sure that a certain amount of coaching goes on."

A defence solicitor in the late interviews had stated that he *did* pre-empt the magistrates' questions and it seems clear that the magistrates were aware of this practice.

The most common comment about engagement between magistrates and defendants from defence solicitors involved in the case studies was that they did not feel that what their client had said had affected the outcome of the case. Only two solicitors thought that their client's comments had affected the sentence. Positive comments about the magistrates' questions included the statement that:

> "Both client and parent were encouraged to focus upon the situation and, particularly in the case of the client, he was not able to distance himself from the proceedings".

The same solicitor also said:

> "The client was given a real opportunity to explain his problems and was encouraged to take a positive approach to the new supervision order."

However other solicitors felt that the magistrates were just going through the motions with their questions. One thought that the magistrates' questions were ineffectual or inane and that it would be hard for children to answer briefly questions such as 'why did you do it?' or 'are you sorry?'.

Techniques of engagement

Initially the courts involved in the Demonstration Project deliberately provided little by way of detailed and specific guidance to magistrates as to what kind of questions to ask defendants and parents. The protocols adopted for both courts stressed that communication between chairmen and defendants should focus on the offender's offending behaviour, and that this discussion should only take place after conviction. Some of the other courts surveyed by telephone took a different approach, however. One court area had adopted a protocol drawn up by a child and adolescent psychiatrist who, for example, gave the following advice:

'Questions should be open where possible. Closed questions that are only answered by 'yes' or 'no' should be avoided – some useful words and phrases are (a) tell us about … (b) How do you feel? (c) What do you think? (d) Who, what, where, when, why, or how?'

At these courts magistrates were also advised that they should avoid being patronising, keep what they say short and simple, and not say anything that the defendant might think they did not mean, such as, 'We're only trying to help you.'

At another of the telephone survey courts, magistrates were told that their two main objectives were:

- to get offenders to understand the seriousness of what they had done in order to get them to take responsibility

- to demonstrate that the court is concerned with the offender as an individual, and to pass a sentence appropriate to the individual offender.

To these ends magistrates were encouraged, as starting points:

- to ask open-ended questions of defendants about the effects of their offences on the victims and about why the defendant became involved in the offence

- to ask defendants to confirm personal information in the pre-sentence report.

In the Demonstration Project courts the approach was less prescriptive, although in Rotherham further guidance was subsequently given in a revised protocol. Even if courts are wary of producing a list of questions for fear that it may lead to routinised questioning, and anticipation by the defence, there may be a case for courts exchanging experiences with each other so that good practice and experience can be disseminated more widely.

One other matter worth referring to is the language used in court. To engage effectively with young people in the courtroom it is important to avoid legal jargon and use language they can understand. During the project the researchers compiled a list of phrases used by court personnel that appeared to be confusing or hard for the young people appearing in court to understand. Examples of these phrases and some suggested alternative formulations are given in Appendix F.

Court observations

Clearly there was a strong perception that magistrates did engage with defendants more as a consequence of the Demonstration Project. However, it is of some interest to consider whether, and in what ways, these perceptions accorded with actual practice. In order to examine court practice, observations were conducted in the courts throughout both phases of the research, involving 1,293 cases (details of the observations are given in Appendix B). Although the observations recorded all the interactions taking place in the courtroom, the main interest was in those involving the magistrates and the defendants. Did magistrates talk more with defendants? Did they ask them more questions? Did they talk to their family more? Did the defendants themselves become involved in talking more? Furthermore, because magistrates are inhibited to some extent in what they can say prior to a finding of guilt, most attention was paid to what engagement occurred in hearings where sentencing took place. It was known from the start of the study that the number of hearings that it would be possible to observe in individual county Youth Courts in Leicestershire would be too few to make it possible to analyse changes occurring at each and every court. However, since participants in the project suggested that there might be important differences between the city and county Youth Courts in Leicestershire, the results for the Leicestershire county courts were grouped together, and the data was examined for Rotherham, Leicester City Youth Court, and the four Leicestershire county Youth Courts.

In answer to the question, 'did magistrates talk more to defendants as the project progressed?' the data from the observations suggested that there were fluctuations in the number of times that magistrates talked to defendants, rather than a clear pattern of increasing engagement, as Figure 3.1 shows:

Figure 3.1:   Mean number of times that magistrates talked to defendants, by court areas and month, for sentencing hearings [1]

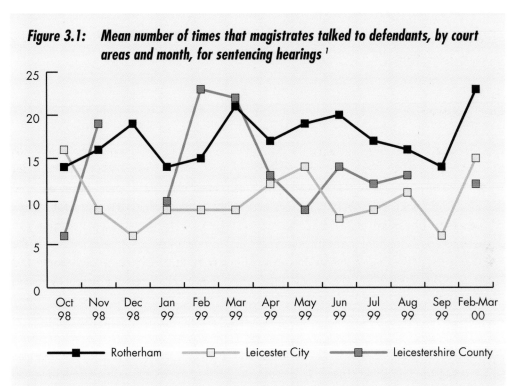

Note:
1.   There were no observations at Leicestershire county courts during December 1998 and September 1999.

It is, however, worth noting that in Rotherham the number of times that magistrates talked to defendants in hearings was higher during the follow-up period (talking 23 times on average) than at any other time, and markedly higher than at the beginning of the project (14 times per case on average during the first month of the project in October 1998; Appendix B, Table B5). One possible explanation for this is that it took a long time for the project to make its impact apparent. However, it is also possible that the follow-up period was no more than another upward fluctuation, rather than an established pattern.

Talking to defendants in general may not carry any great importance. But did magistrates seek to engage defendants to a greater extent by asking more *questions* following the start of the project?

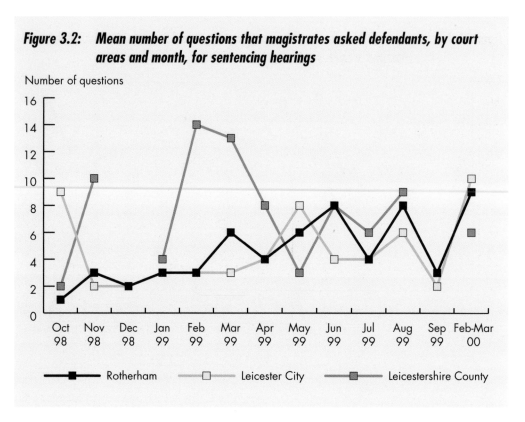

Figure 3.2: **Mean number of questions that magistrates asked defendants, by court areas and month, for sentencing hearings**

Figure 3.2 suggests that, as before, there was no consistent upward trend, although again Rotherham asked a higher mean number of questions during the follow-up period than at the beginning of the project (9 per case on average during February and March 2000 compared with just one per case in October 1998). Leicester city Youth Court had small peaks, and Leicestershire county Youth Courts had a more noticeable peak during the spring of 1999, which coincided with sessions to give magistrates some training in engaging with young offenders.

It is possible that just looking at the means conceals a different kind of effect. We were told that quite often in the past magistrates did not ask defendants questions at all, so it may be that it was not the average amount of questioning that changed, but the fact that magistrates would be likely to ask questions at all. Figure 3.3 shows the proportion of occasions in a particular month when magistrates asked offenders no questions.

Figure 3.3: **Percentage of cases in which magistrates asked defendants no questions, by court areas and month, for sentencing hearings**

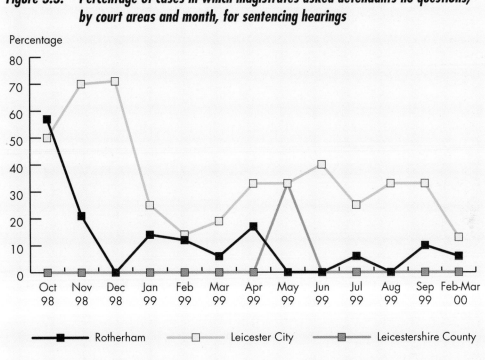

Here, there does appear to be a trend emerging, although various interpretations are possible. In Rotherham in more than half the sentenced cases dealt with at the beginning of the project in October 1998, the magistrates did not ask the young offender any questions; but there then appeared to be an immediate impact resulting in a drop to less than a fifth of all sentenced cases involving no questions. However, because it was not possible to obtain a baseline of what happened prior to the start of the project it is not known to what extent October 1998 was typical of pre-project practice. In Leicester there was a similar decline in the proportion of cases in which magistrates asked no questions after December 1998, although not to such a low level as in Rotherham. This could be accounted for in a variety of ways, such as a small proportion of magistrates in a large city court not becoming as involved in the new practices as the majority of their colleagues. In the county Youth Courts in Leicestershire, by contrast, it appears that throughout the study period magistrates asked at least one question when sentencing young offenders. This may be because, as mentioned earlier, there was already an established practice of questioning young offenders prior to the instigation of the project, but without pre-project data it is not possible to know this for certain. One further qualification to be noted is that the data in Figure 3.3 sometimes involved quite small numbers. For example, the peak in the county Youth Courts in Leicestershire in May 1999 when no questions were asked involved just two cases.

A further consideration is whether encouraging magistrates to engage more directly in court also extended to them making more enquiries of young offenders' families. In Leicester magistrates did ask significantly more questions of offenders' families in April 1999 than in November and December 1998, but otherwise there was no evidence of any change in the extent to which the questioning of defendants' families by magistrates changed.

An aspect of the project that attracted considerable support from magistrates and others working in the Youth Court was the idea that the young offender should no longer be a passive observer of proceedings. Therefore did offenders talk more in court? The results are not unequivocal, but in Rotherham and Leicester the amount that young offenders talked in the course of sentencing hearings was higher during the follow-up period than at any time since the start of the project. In the county courts in Leicestershire the amount of talking by young offenders during the follow-up period was twice what it had been at the start of the project, but not as great as it had been during February to April 1999, suggesting that, as with the number of questions that magistrates asked offenders (Figure 3.2), offender involvement peaked around the time that training courses were taking place (Figure 3.4).

Figure 3.4: **Mean number of times that defendants talked, by court areas and month, for sentencing hearings**

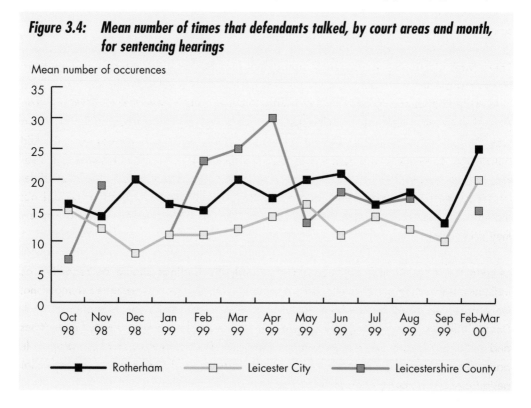

Mean number of occurences

Rotherham — Leicester City — Leicestershire County

At the beginning of the project some concern had been expressed that if magistrates did engage more with defendants then this might result in longer hearings, at a time when courts were being urged to deal with cases as swiftly as possible and reduce delay in the system. In Rotherham the length of hearings did vary to some extent between different months during the period of the Demonstration Project, but there was no consistent pattern, and the variations seemed rather to indicate large fluctuations in the times of hearings rather than any effect attributable to the project itself. There were no significant differences in the length of hearings between any two months during the period of the Demonstration Project in Leicestershire.

To summarise then, in hearings where young offenders were sentenced, there was no clearly identifiable and consistent pattern suggesting that, in general, magistrates talked to young offenders more following the start of the project, or asked them or their families more questions on average. However, there were indications that changes did take place. Although the average *amount* of questions did not increase in a consistent manner, the occasions on which magistrates asked *no* questions decreased, suggesting that it was not so much that there was an overall increase in questioning, as that magistrates did at least ask some questions where previously they might have asked none.

There was also some evidence that (apart from the Youth Courts in the county in Leicestershire) young offenders participated by talking more than hitherto. It was also noticeable that where changes did occur they were most in evidence during the follow-up period, suggesting that it may have taken some time for any shift in approach to work its way through. Despite the project's objective of encouraging greater engagement, this did not appear to result in any general increase in the length of time that hearings lasted. This is encouraging if courts are also expected to deal with cases as speedily as possible, and it is consistent with the indications that the overall amount of questioning did not increase, but rather that magistrates may have asked one or two questions where previously they asked none.

Despite the large number of hearings observed, the findings should be regarded as indicative rather than conclusive. This is because it is hard to know whether the changes that were observed could be attributed directly to the impact of the Demonstration Project. Despite differences being statistically significant, it is possible that they reflected fluctuations and variability in practice rather than a cause and effect consequence of the project. In particular, there were no baseline data, so comparisons could not be made with a similar period preceding the initiation of the project.

Evaluating engagement

All aspects of the research suggest that encouraging magistrates to engage directly with young offenders and their families was a popular, and largely successful, aspect of the Demonstration Project. It appears to have made magistrates more confident that they were sentencing defendants to punishments that were right for them, and there were also indications that in certain cases engagement influenced the sentence arrived at by magistrates (further reference is made to this in Chapter 7). Engagement did not seem to increase the length of court hearings, although some magistrates indicated that they cut back on engagement if the court list was busy. In addition, engagement appears to have made magistrates look critically at the language they used in court, to make sure that it was understandable by defendants (this is important in the light of a practice direction issued by the Lord Chief Justice in relation to the Crown Court in February 2000, which is considered further in Chapter 8). Although engagement appears to have been accepted in both areas, there were some remaining concerns. One was that defence solicitors would pre-empt engagement by magistrates by anticipating their questions. Another was that magistrates needed more training than had initially been allowed for in the early stages of the Demonstration Project, and more practical advice on engaging with young offenders and their families in order to be as effective as possible. A protocol produced in Rotherham giving magistrates further guidance on engagement was felt to have been useful.

4   The court environment

Changes to court layout

The Youth Court in Rotherham started to experiment with the layout of the court in a limited way soon after the project started. From November 1998 parents, who had previously sat behind their children, sat next to them in court. In February 1999 more substantial changes were introduced. The magistrates moved from sitting on quite a high bench to sitting in the well of the court, and the remaining desks in the courtroom were combined with the magistrates' desk to produce a circular pattern. Defendants and their parents had their own desk between Youth Justice workers and their solicitor. The witness box was initially part of this circle, but was soon removed to provide more room, and in trials witnesses sat at a desk in the circle. In addition, lawyers and members of other organisations were asked to remain seated when they addressed the bench. Defendants were allowed to sit when being questioned, but were still expected to stand when being identified and when sentences or adjournments were announced. The changes to the layout in Rotherham were, however, only introduced in one of the courtrooms used by the Youth Court. The other courtroom was used only rarely, and its layout stayed in the traditional style.

Following the introduction of the new layout some alterations were made in the ensuing weeks as a result of experience. Desks were moved closer together or further apart to make the agencies in court feel more comfortable. In addition, although magistrates initially moved back onto the raised bench to hear the cases of defendants in custody, they soon decided to remain in the well of the court to deal with these cases also. From May 1999 the magistrates were provided with an extra desk so that they were not cramped together behind one desk, and members of the Youth Justice team moved from the circle of desks to a desk at the back corner of the court. This was to allow more room for the other parties in the court. As the project progressed magistrates also allowed defendants to sit when being identified and sentenced as well as at other times.

In all courts in Leicestershire lawyers and members of other organisations were requested to remain seated while making representations to the bench, but because the court architecture was so different in the various locations each court developed its own arrangements for making changes to the layout of the courtroom. These are described below.

Leicester City court

In this city court minor changes were made to the court layouts in January 1999, with defendants' desks moved closer to the bench, and a presumption that parents should sit with their children if possible. In March 1999 more substantial changes were made. Court 10 changed only slightly, the defendant's desk being moved nearer to the bench and the witness box being moved to reduce any likelihood of an intimidating appearance. Subsequently, however, the witness box was returned to its original position, as it was found that this was the only way in which witnesses could sit and give evidence in comfort. In Court 9, however, the magistrates moved to sit in the well of the court. The layout of the desks in Court 9 was also changed, and by the end of April 1999 the desks were arranged in a rectangular shape. In addition, the witness box was removed and witnesses sat at a desk in the rectangle instead. In October 1999 magistrates in Court 9 moved back onto the bench to create more room in the court and allow victims to sit at a desk further away from the defendant and closer to the magistrates. The desks in the court remained in a roughly rectangular shape, although the defendants' desk was moved slightly closer to the magistrates.

Market Bosworth court

The magistrates moved into the well of the court in January 1999, and desks were moved into a rectangular layout, with magistrates and defendants sitting opposite each other. By May 1999 the table that defendants sat at was moved closer to the bench so that the court was no longer in a strict rectangular shape. Throughout the project witnesses continued to give evidence from the witness box, which was placed behind the defendant so that defendants could not see the witness when the witness was giving evidence. After May 1999 minor changes were made to try to give magistrates and the Crown Prosecutors more space because, like other occupants of the courtroom, they were seated very close together. Since a move to a new courthouse was planned for January 2000 the changes put into place for the project were viewed as temporary. When the move to the new courthouse occurred the magistrates could sit in two courtrooms. Both had the desks set out in a rectangle and the magistrates sat in the well of the court. In these courtrooms witnesses gave evidence from a desk in the rectangle. Unlike the previous courthouse there was adequate room for all parties and for people to move around the courtroom. In addition one of the courtrooms had a perspex screen away from the main part of the courtroom for defendants in custody, giving increased security.

Ashby de la Zouch court

Ashby de la Zouch court had an old courtroom with fixed furniture, so it was impossible to change the court layout. Some consideration was given to using one of the magistrates' retiring rooms as an informal courtroom for the project, but this did not find any favour amongst the magistrates. Because of the limitations on changing the physical environment magistrates at this court decided to concentrate on using more verbal means of making the court feel less formal instead.

Loughborough court

By January 1999 the Youth Court was experimenting with several different layouts in its three courtrooms, so that final arrangements could be chosen by March 1999. After March, the three courtrooms were set out so that proceedings took place in the well of the court. All courtrooms had a rectangular layout, with witnesses giving their evidence from a desk in the rectangle. Two courtrooms stayed like this throughout the project, but in April 1999 one of the smaller courtrooms reverted to magistrates sitting on the bench as previously since the room was too small for court staff to feel comfortable.

Melton Mowbray court

Melton Mowbray Court experimented with a number of different layouts. The Youth Court was initially set out in a horseshoe shape, then a rectangle, and finally in a 'H' formation. The 'H' formation proved popular because defendants were closer to the magistrates. The magistrates experimented with sitting in the well, but decided to move back onto the bench.

In studying the different arrangements we have made reference to three main types of layout: "traditional", "alternative" and "well". "Traditional" means that the magistrates were seated on the bench, with the court laid out traditionally, as all the courts started out originally. "Alternative" means that the magistrates were seated on the bench, but that there had been changes to the rest of the courtroom. This included Court 10 at Leicester City Court, and the courts in Loughborough and Melton Mowbray where magistrates remained on the bench but the rest of the court was set out in a rectangle or an 'H' shape. In Rotherham it refers to two cases where the court was set out in the well of the court, but magistrates moved back onto the bench to hear the case of a defendant in custody. "Well" means that, in addition to other changes, the magistrates sat in the well of the court to hear cases.

Views of the changes

Changing the court environment was an aspect of the Demonstration Project that resulted in some differing opinions. In the initial interviews with court personnel, clerks and social workers appeared to be quite positive about changing the layout of courtrooms, whilst magistrates and crown prosecutors were more likely to be against it, though by no means all of them. One thing that most interviewees were agreed on was that the dignity of the court had to be preserved, and another concern was whether a layout that appeared to be more 'informal' would affect security. It was felt by some people that defendants would not respect a more informal court, and that a formal court served to curb defendants' "baser instincts", as one person put it. There was a view that an informal court would be most appropriate for first time or younger offenders. However, the practicalities of assessing the 'non-risk' and 'risk' offenders, and listing them in different courts, or moving the courts around to accommodate them, was seen as problematic.

In the second round of interviews in the summer of 1999, the change in court environment was the aspect of the project that, along with engagement, was identified as having affected the court and people's jobs the most. It was also the most controversial. Although the magistrates who were interviewed tended to be positive about the changes to court layout, saying that it had helped to facilitate increased engagement in the courtroom, they were also the magistrates who were most likely to have played a part in introducing the changes brought about by the project. Lawyers tended to be more negative about the effect of the new layout, commenting on the lack of space in some courts (such as Market Bosworth), and the lack of focus on the offender in the courts that had a more 'informal' appearance (such as Leicester City). Youth Justice workers were more encouraging about the layout, one worker in Rotherham saying that the layout had encouraged *everyone* to talk more in court, not just magistrates. Concerns about the court environment included the lack of space in some of the Leicestershire courts, and the effect that this could have on victims and witnesses attending court who tended to be "within hitting or spitting distance at trials". There was also some concern that 'informality', particularly sitting down to address the bench, was not appropriate in certain circumstances, such as bail applications and sentencing hearings.

Court staff had a lot to say about how the new layouts had affected their jobs. Lawyers felt that the new layout and the fact that they were expected to sit down affected the quality of their advocacy. It was also felt that it was hard to move between the adult and youth courts and follow the different rules. A positive comment came from a court clerk in Rotherham, who stated that, although he acknowledged it made magistrates uncomfortable, the new layout meant that when he was giving the magistrates advice it was more open to the rest of the court, which he felt was better. Generally, the court staff acknowledged that the envisioned security problems had not materialised.

There was a belief amongst interviewees that the change in layout had had some effect on defendants. However, there were mixed opinions as to what exactly this had been. There was some debate as to whether the change of layout made defendants feel more comfortable so that they could participate more fully (especially in relation to trials), or whether it had led defendants to lose respect for the court.

Seventy-one per cent of comments about changes in the layout in the court logbooks were unfavourable (20 positive, 55 negative, 2 neutral). However, it should be borne in mind that those who were unhappy about the arrangements might well be the ones most likely to write a comment in the book, whereas those who were happy with the new layout would be less likely to make any comment. Furthermore, some of the adverse comments on the new layouts could be considered to refer to 'teething problems'. There were references to specific arrangements about who sat where which were subsequently changed. There were also suggestions in the logbooks that some magistrates, while unhappy with sitting on the same level as defendants, might be willing to accept a layout whereby the magistrates sat on a dais which was slightly raised by a few inches, as happened at another court not involved in the Demonstration Project, but included in the telephone survey.

In the questionnaire distributed to all those involved in the work of the Youth Court in the summer of 1999, respondents were asked to say how satisfactory they thought the changes to the layout and use of the court had been, rating them 'good', 'satisfactory' or 'unsatisfactory' (with 'good' scoring 1 and 'unsatisfactory' scoring 3, so that the lower score has a higher rating). Table 4.1 shows the mean ratings and the rankings for the various changes.

Table 4.1:   Satisfaction with court layout

	All respondents		Magistrates only	
	mean score	ranking	mean score	ranking
Where defendants sit	2.09	1	1.98	1
Where solicitors sit	2.13	2	2.07	2
Sitting down more	2.14	3	2.17	4
Where others sit	2.23	4	2.19	5
Where witnesses sit	2.24	5	2.10	3
Where magistrates sit	2.32	6	2.50	6

From this it can be seen that the least unpopular change was that to where defendants sat, and the most unpopular was where magistrates sat. Another question specifically asked respondents whether they thought magistrates should sit on the same or a different level to defendants. Two-thirds of all respondents (67%) thought magistrates should be on a different level to defendants, with just over seven out of every ten magistrates (72%) thinking this. There were no significant differences between Rotherham and Leicestershire regarding responses to the changes.

One of the initial concerns about changes to the layout of the Youth Court was whether it would affect the security of the court adversely. In replying to the questionnaire the majority of magistrates (55%) and others (59%) thought that security had remained unchanged, although a noticeable minority (39% of magistrates and 32% of others) thought that the court was less secure since the project started. It is worth noting that the researchers were not made aware of any noticeable lapses in security during the course of the project which resulted in people absconding, causing damage or attacking other people.

A further questionnaire was distributed in February 2000, during the follow-up period. In both court areas the majority of respondents now thought that in courts where the layout had been changed since the project started the changes were good or satisfactory, with the non-magistrates being more likely to think this than magistrates. Again respondents were asked about different aspects of the changes, covering where magistrates, defendants, solicitors and others sat, and about the fact that business was now conducted sitting down more. In every instance the majority opinion was that the changes were good or satisfactory. The results of the follow-up survey appear to indicate a move towards being more prepared to accept the changes, compared with the initial survey.

Respondents were asked about the different types of layout in operation during the course of the Demonstration Project ("Traditional", "Alternative" and "Well", as explained in the opening section of this chapter). The majority said that they found all three types to be good or satisfactory, with the exception of the Leicestershire justices, a majority of whom found the 'Well' type of layout to be unsatisfactory. This is shown in Table 4.2, which omits those respondents who said that they were unable to express an opinion.

Table 4.2: *Percentage of respondents expressing an opinion who said they found a particular layout to be 'Good' or 'Satisfactory'*

	Magistrates	Others	ALL
a) 'Notional' Layout			
Rotherham	77	79	78
Leicestershire	89	76	85
b) 'Alternative' Layout			
Rotherham	87	74	79
Leicestershire	88	83	86
c) 'Well' Layout			
Rotherham	59	65	62
Leicestershire	40	56	45

It is possible that there were differences within Leicestershire between the various court locations, but it was not possible to make such differentiations within the present data set.

One of the main reasons for doing a follow-up of the initial evaluation of the Demonstration Project was to see whether opinions changed once participants had had more time to become familiar with the new measures. Consequently respondents were asked whether their opinion of the new layouts had changed in the six months between the end of the initial evaluation and the follow-up. In both areas about half of the respondents said that their opinions had not changed, but amongst those who did change their views the shift was towards being more in favour of the new layouts. Eliminating those who answered "I can't say", more than a third in Rotherham and four out of ten in Leicestershire said that they were now more prepared to accept the new layouts, which is consistent with the results reported earlier. The pattern was similar for magistrates and for others who worked in the Youth Court, with the 'others' having shifted somewhat more in favour than the magistrates.

In Rotherham just over half of all respondents in the follow-up survey (53%) who expressed a view felt that the changes in court layout brought about by the Demonstration Project had been beneficial, whereas in Leicestershire the majority (54%) thought that they had had little impact. There was little difference between magistrates and others in either area.

During the follow-up period it was said by all but four of those interviewed that the months between September 1999 and February 2000 had given people a chance to get used to the new layouts. Twenty-two of the 28 people interviewed reported that the changes in layout had become part of the everyday running of the Youth Court.

Case studies

Interviews with those involved in the cases studied in some detail sought to discover whether defendants who had been in court previously noticed any change in the court environment after the Demonstration Project was introduced. Twenty-seven of the 39 defendants interviewed had previous convictions. Eight of these noticed no difference between their past and present court experiences. This even included one defendant whose case was heard in the well of the court. On his last appearance the magistrates had sat on the bench, but he did not realise that they had moved, even when this was explained to him. Although the number of cases studies was few, this suggests that the change of environment had little or no effect on some defendants.

The most common differences noted by defendants were that the magistrates were asking more questions, and that the layout in court had changed. A number of defendants said that the 'well' layout made them feel more comfortable and this made it easier to talk to the magistrates. However, three people said that the court should not be informal (this included defendants who said that they had felt better in the new layout). One defendant in Rotherham said, "The magistrates should sit at the top and make people scared". Another stated that the fact that he could see the bench behind the magistrates made him think that they were not proper magistrates because they were not sat up there. Another was concerned for the safety of magistrates, saying "they're better off sitting right away from the person in court". This suggests that at least some defendants felt the court should retain a stern image. However, one defendant felt that the 'informal' layout in Loughborough court was "scarier" than a formal layout in Leicester City court because the magistrates were looking at him more.

Families of defendants who had been in court before noticed that they were now sitting with their children, and that magistrates were asking more questions. The overall feeling was that sitting next to their child was a positive development and enabled them to support their child more. The movement of magistrates from the bench into the well of the court was also seen as a positive move. A mother who was interviewed at Market Bosworth court said that she could now look *at* the magistrates rather than *up* to them. Before she had felt as though *she* had done something wrong.

Before any changes were made to the layout of the court there were mixed opinions about the prospect of change amongst magistrates interviewed in the case studies, particularly regarding security. After changes to the layout were made most of the magistrates (58%) who sat in the well of the court said they did not think that the change in layout had affected the outcome of the case they had been dealing with. Magistrates were positive about parents being seated next to their children, as this meant that parents could be more supportive of their child and take a more active part in the proceedings. At all the courts involved in the project there was concern that moving into the well of the court had left the courtroom short of space. Just after they moved into the well of the court magistrates in Rotherham complained that the court was "like a supper party". One magistrate said about the court in Loughborough that "the layout in that particular courtroom today was slightly claustrophobic. I think people were in much too close proximity". A few magistrates also said that they did not like the solicitors sitting down to address them.

However, there was a feeling that the changes were making it easier for defendants to talk:

'If we'd have been up there [on the bench] I think that [the defendant would] have been an awful lot more intimidated.'

Another magistrate said:

'It helps the defendant if they can sit down ... even if they're quite hardened I think there's still value ... I think it does help them speak.'

It was also felt in Rotherham that the new layout encouraged eye contact between defendants and magistrates:

'As I'm sat down and I'm on a level with them at least they have tended, today, to keep eye contact with me and concentrate.'

The feeling amongst defence solicitors before any changes were made to the court layout was that the court should remain as it was. Again, there were security concerns. After the changes were made, solicitors said they did not think that the different layout had had any effect on their clients' cases. Some thought that the court was too friendly. However, one solicitor said that the informal court had particularly helped his client. Only one solicitor said that he liked sitting to address the bench. Some solicitors did not like the fact that their clients were being seated with their parents. Reasons for this ranged from it making the defendant more reluctant to speak, to a belief that it was better if defendants sat on their own because this focused attention on them. One solicitor said that it should be decided whether the purpose of the court was to punish defendants or solve their problems before considering how the court should be set out.

Indications from court observations

Some people mentioned the possibility that the introduction of new layouts might facilitate better communication between magistrates and defendants. This is hard to evaluate because new layouts only came into operation once the project had been underway for some time, so there could well have been a correlation between new layouts and greater engagement, but one brought about by the training and encouragement to engage which had taken place, rather than by the court layout itself.

Nonetheless data from the court observations was analysed to see whether there was at least an association between different layouts and the likelihood of magistrates asking questions more, and defendants talking more, even if the relationship was not necessarily a causal one. Table 4.3 shows the mean number of questions that magistrates asked defendants for the different types of layout referred to earlier.

Table 4.3: *Mean number of questions that magistrates asked defendants, by court areas and layout, for sentencing hearings*

	Rotherham	Leicestershire City	Leicestershire County
Traditional	3.7	2.6	8.9
Alternative	n/a	5.6	8.0
Well	6.2	4.8	6.2

The only difference that was statistically significant was in Rotherham, between the traditional layout and the magistrates sitting in the well of the court ($t = 3.87$, $p < .001$). No other differences were apparent, for example in the number of times the defendant talked, and for the reason mentioned earlier very little can be inferred from the difference in Rotherham.

Another consideration was whether different court layouts affected the likelihood of magistrates retiring more to discuss the case. Some magistrates had said that they felt they had to retire more when they sat in the well of the court, because they did not feel as comfortable discussing matters in such close proximity to others in court. However, analyses did not reveal any significant difference in the number of retirements as a result of different layouts. In Rotherham 28 per cent of cases heard in the traditional court layout resulted in at least one retirement, whereas when magistrates sat in the well of the court the comparable figure was 24 per cent. Cases were slightly, though not significantly, more likely to involve two retirements in the 'well' layout (3% of cases compared with 1% in the traditional setting). In Leicestershire in hearings where magistrates sat in the well of the court, more cases did involve at least one retirement (38% compared to 31% in the traditional setting, and 33% in the alternative layout). In general, however, there appeared to be no relationship between the movement of magistrates into the well of the court and an increase in the number of retirements.

Evaluating changes to the court environment

It would be fair to say that, initially at least, the response to changing the court layout was mixed amongst magistrates and court staff, with those most involved with the project being more positive. The concern that what was generally viewed as a more 'informal' court layout could lead to security problems does not appear to have materialised, and moving the desks in the court into a rectangle or circular shape does not appear to have been contentious. It was the moving of magistrates into the well of the court that caused most concern. This was partly a practical consideration, in that the movement of magistrates into the well of the court often made the courtrooms feel very cramped and participants often felt as though they were too close to one another, especially where victims and witnesses were attending trials and sentencing hearings. There were also problems with fitting a large number of co-defendants and their families together in court. The main source of these problems is a consequence of losing a significant amount of the available space taken up by the raised bench. If magistrates do adopt the practice of sitting in the well of the court, then some thought may need to be given to reclaiming the space taken up by the unused benches. The other concern was that a move into the well of the court would introduce more informality and lead to the Youth Court losing some of its dignity and authority. Several magistrates and court staff felt that the court should represent a stern response to offending behaviour, and some of the defendants who were interviewed also took this view.

Apart from specific concerns, the alterations to the courtroom were felt by court users to have had more impact on their daily working environment than any other aspect of the Demonstration Project. This was because it effectively changed the ethos within which they were operating. As well as getting used to new spatial arrangements, it was more difficult for those working in the court to maintain the kind of distance and formality to which they were accustomed. Apart from the court being more open, the participants also had to act in a more open manner themselves; for example, it was mentioned by several participants that it was not so easy for magistrates and others to engage in whispered asides. Some people welcomed this, whereas others did not, but there were indications that people did become more accustomed to it as time went by.

Throughout the project there was recognition that the Youth Court covers a wide range of defendants in terms of age, experience and seriousness of offence and there was an acceptance that in general the Youth Court should not appear to be intimidating towards younger and less experienced defendants. This last point was reinforced by a Practice Direction from the Lord Chief Justice in early 2000,[2] as a result of a European Court of Human Rights ruling, which said that, 'The trial should, if practicable, be held in a courtroom in which all the participants were on the same level or almost the same level' (para.9), and 'A young defendant should normally, if he wishes, be free to sit with members of his family or others in a place which permits easy, informal communication with his legal representatives and others with whom he wants or needs to communicate' (para.10). Although this Direction applies to the Crown Court rather than the Youth Court, it has implications for the way in which young defendants are dealt with in general and is likely to promote further the moves initiated by the Demonstration Project. The Practice Direction is considered further in Chapter 8.

2   [2000] 2 All ER 285.

5   Opening up the Youth Court: involving victims and the press

Attendance by victims

Prior to the Demonstration Project, there was little attendance by victims in the Youth Courts in either area, apart from appearing as witnesses in a trial. In early interviews and meetings many people expressed agreement with the principle of encouraging victims to attend court, but also foresaw practical difficulties that would need to be resolved. These practical concerns included who would look after victims, where they would wait and whether victims should be allowed to stay in court when delicate information was being discussed. Magistrates were most likely to be positive about admitting victims, whilst defence solicitors were most likely to be against the idea. A common view was that while victims had a right to know what happened in court, coming to court itself was perhaps not the best way of finding out. The effect upon defendants of seeing victims in court was unknown, but it was feared that it might act as a barrier against engaging with them. A lot of interviewees believed that victims would be reluctant to come to court, and may be upset by the experience.

In Rotherham the local police were advised that there would be a presumption that victims could attend court, although the final decision about attendance in any given case would be made by the magistrates. Victims attended the Youth Court in 11 of the 670 cases observed during the first year of the research. Most of these victims were related to the offender and had come to court to support them. Twelve victims attended out of 623 cases observed in Leicestershire Youth Courts during the first year of the project and, as in Rotherham, most were related to the defendant and were appearing in court as their support; otherwise the victims were in court as witnesses in trials. The Project Board in Leicestershire agreed that Leicester City Court would take the lead in inviting victims to attend court. Consequently the police and Victim Support considered how best to inform victims about cases. This involved naming defendants in letters to victims so that it would be easier for them to find the relevant case if they came to court. However, their legal advisors informed the police in Leicestershire that they could not name defendants in such letters. This contrasted with the advice that Rotherham police were given. In addition, an oversight meant that until September 1999 victims in Leicester received letters stating that they could *not* attend court. An amended letter was drafted which advised victims that they could attend court if they wished. The Project Board in Leicestershire also discussed the possibility of encouraging victims present as witnesses in trials to remain in court to see how the offender was sentenced, and this message was passed to the county benches.

In the cases that were observed where victims attended, the main issue raised by participants was the proximity of victims to offenders in the courtroom, particularly as layouts in the well of the court decreased the amount of space available in the courtroom. In some courts victims who wished to attend hearings were seated very close to offenders or the offenders' family, and there were cases where defendants maintained unsettling eye contact with victims or witnesses whilst they gave their evidence. Victim Support in both court areas expressed concern at this situation and said that victims and witnesses reported feeling intimidated in courtrooms. Both rectangular and circular layouts generated this problem. In relation to encouraging victims to stay in court after trials, few victims chose to stay in court when they were invited to do so.

Two young victims who attended court were interviewed in Leicestershire. The first (in September 1999) had been hit by the offender during an episode that led to the offender being convicted of a single person affray. The victim and his mother first came to court for a trial in which the defendant pleaded guilty at the last minute, and were invited by the magistrates to return to court to see the offender sentenced. However, when they came back to court the pre-sentence report had not been prepared, the offender was not sentenced, and the magistrates again invited them back to the next hearing. This case illustrates the possibility that victims may take time to come to court and see little, or nothing, happen. Interviewed after the hearing, the victim's mother said she felt that it had been nerve racking in court, and both she and her son disliked the fact that they had had to sit behind the offender. They felt uncomfortable that when the offender left court, he had walked around them. In addition, the victim had been worried about walking out of court, in case something else happened between him and the offender. However, the victim's mother said that she had wanted to know what would happen to the offender, and now she knew that *something* would happen she felt all right. Although the visit to court had reassured her that the offender would be punished, the victim and his mother said they would not come back for the next hearing, as this one had been too traumatic; the Witness Support Service would call them with the result.

The second victim interviewed was a witness in a trial at Leicester City Court in September 1999. Mid-way through the trial the CPS withdrew the charges. Interviewed about the court experience, the victim said he had felt uncomfortable whilst giving his evidence because the defendant was seated close to him and had been staring at him throughout the proceedings. He would have preferred to sit in a position where he could not see the defendant. However, he did not feel that the rectangular shape of the court had been a problem, and said the magistrates sitting in the well of the court had made him feel comfortable giving his evidence. If the case had led to the defendant being sentenced, the victim said that he would have been happy to come back to court to see this.

In the cases observed during the follow-up period victims were seen in court in six cases. These victims were either giving evidence at trial or were related to the defendant and had come to court with them as an appropriate adult. In addition, in two cases in Leicestershire victims attended the court with the intention of persuading the Crown Prosecution Service to drop charges. Although these victims were in the courthouse they were not invited to view the proceedings. In hearings where victims attended court as witnesses they were often invited to stay in court to view the rest of the case. Some victims did take the opportunity to remain in court. One who stayed to see the magistrates' verdict was left on her own in court during the magistrates' retirement to decide upon the defendant's guilt, and was told that she could not remain for sentencing but had to leave the courtroom after the magistrates had found the defendant guilty. In Leicestershire the victim of a car theft and her father (a witness in the case) were interviewed at court after they had given evidence. Throughout their evidence the father of the defendant had been snorting at what they had said. The victim felt that they would have been better off in another court where they were further away from the defendant so they could not hear any comments. She said she had felt fine in the courtroom, but neither she nor her father had liked the fact that the defendant was so close.

Although no victims attended court in any of the case studies, defendants were asked whether they would have minded if the victim of their offence had attended court. The majority of defendants for whom there was a victim in their case, said that they either would not be bothered or would be happy for the victim of their offence to come to court and see them sentenced (23 of 34 defendants). One said:

"I wouldn't have minded; I'd have understood. I'd want to go to court if someone did that to me. I'd want to be in court to see what's going on."

Eight said that they would not want the victim in court, and three did not know. One defendant was worried that if the victim saw his face he would think, "I'll get him". A few defendants still felt antagonistic towards the victim:

"If I was in the same room as him, I'd end up throwing something at him – I can't stand him."

In one case the victim was the defendant's mother, and the defendant said that she would not want her mum there because she would not want to say things that would later make them row.

The supporters of defendants were split between those who felt that the victim should and should not attend court. One mother said:

"I'd have liked them to be there to see them face to face – I think it would worry him if they were there."

However, another said that she would not want the victim to be in court because she would feel ashamed and embarrassed, and another thought that the victim would be gloating at the punishment her son received. One parent was happy for the victim to be in court, but was concerned that something would need to be done before court to separate defendants and victims otherwise they could argue.

Thirty-one benches of magistrates commented on whether they would have admitted the victim of a case study offence into court. Eighty-four per cent of magistrates would have had no objections to them attending. Three benches of magistrates could not agree, and two benches said they would not agree to the victim attending. In one case, this was because it was felt this would have an adverse effect on the defendant, and in the other because the victims were young themselves. Even though the majority of magistrates would have no objection to victims attending, they did recognise some potential problems. It was believed that some victims might not want to come to court, such as large stores whose goods had been shoplifted. There was also concern that victims would not be happy with the sentence given, particularly if the amount of compensation was small because of the offender's limited means. There was also concern about where victims would sit, and that they may not understand the court's reasons for what it did because they would not have access to a pre-sentence report.

None of the defence solicitors interviewed would have wanted the victim of their client's offence to attend court. Reasons included concern that the victim would intervene during the case, or that provocation by the victim was being used as defence mitigation. There was also concern that it would not be in their client's interest, and that personal problems might be discussed.

Most of the court personnel interviewed in the summer of 1999, towards the end of the first phase of the project had had no experience of victims being in court during the time the project had been in operation. The issue was still considered problematic in terms of getting victims to court, and ensuring that they did not have unrealistic expectations of what might happen. The limited space available in the courtrooms, especially where new layouts had been adopted, was also a concern. One defence solicitor in Rotherham had had the experience of a victim turning up for one of her client's cases and although she had initially been quite positive about the idea of victims attending court, in this case it had caused her client distress and she was no longer so supportive of the idea. In response to the questionnaire circulated to all those who worked in the Youth Court in the summer of 1999, most people (63% of all respondents and 72% of magistrates) thought that the project had made little impact on the likelihood of victims attending court, and this was the view that was most in evidence in response to the follow-up questionnaire sent out in February 2000. Despite the lack of attendance by victims, most of those interviewed during the follow-up period in March 2000 thought that victims should continue to be encouraged to attend the Youth Court if they wished.

Attendance by the press

There was widespread agreement in both areas that prior to the Demonstration Project the press rarely, if ever, attended court. Leicester City Court had had a court reporter in the past, but newspapers could not now afford to have a reporter assigned to the courts. It was felt that the press might come to the Youth Court more if offenders could be named, but those who worked in the Youth Court thought that reporters would only come to court for the more dramatic and salacious stories. In Rotherham a local newspaper wrote an initial story about the Demonstration Project when Rotherham first became involved in it. There were no specific initiatives in Rotherham to involve the press more closely in what was happening as a result of the project and, although the local press were aware of the project, their presence in court was the result of high profile cases, such as local arson, manslaughter and attempted murder, rather than a response to the court opening up. The Project Board in Leicestershire decided that local newspapers would be most likely to attend the court in the main city, and therefore Leicester City Court would be best placed for a deliberate attempt to interest the press in the work of the Youth Court. Consequently Leicester City Court initiated discussions with the city newspaper, as a result of which the newspaper agreed to place a reporter in the Youth Court every day that it sat for a trial period of three months, beginning in April 1999. The reporter was provided with a seat in the courtrooms and the court and supplemental lists. After the trial period the newspaper decided to keep a presence in the court, but to reduce it to once a week. Of the 65 articles published in the local paper during the project initiative, 48 were court reports, and a further 14 were articles about the Youth Court and youth justice in general. The remaining three articles were editorials, and there was also an unrecorded number of letters from the public about the Youth Court and related issues.

The court reports tended to concentrate on the most serious offences and sentences. Violent offences (including murder and attempted murder) made up about a third of the court reports. Property offences were also widely covered, making up 19 of the reports. Thirty of the court reports mentioned that the offender had been sentenced, and in half of these the offender had received a custodial sentence. In general, reports provided a balanced view of cases, often including quotations from defence solicitors and points of mitigation as well as the prosecution case and magistrates' comments. Court reports also recorded apologies that offenders had made to their victims and abuse that offenders themselves had suffered.

Of the 14 articles about youth justice and the courts during the initial research period, five were about the project itself. These were mostly about the issue of naming and shaming, and one polled city residents about their opinions of lifting reporting restrictions. There were also articles about fast-tracking persistent young offenders, curfew orders and other aspects of the Crime and Disorder Act 1998, secure remand procedures, and an article about how offenders under ten years of age were dealt with. Although attendance by a city reporter was reduced from three days to one day a week after the initial three months trial period, the paper appeared to continue to find the stories a valuable part of its news and current affairs coverage. Apart from the initiative at Leicester City Court, reporters appeared in the county Youth Courts in Leicestershire during the period of the project but, as in Rotherham, this appeared to be in response to occasional 'interesting' cases, or because they had come to see a case in the adult court which had been adjourned, as a consequence of which they 'wandered into' the Youth Court. The reporter from the local paper at Leicester City Court who had been in court for the three-month trial period was interviewed during the follow-up period. She had not been in court often since the trial period because this had been down the list of priorities for the newspaper and they did not have enough reporters. Usually agency reporters covered the court. Although the trial period had been interesting the stories had become repetitious after a while and were of less interest if the young person concerned could not be named. She added that in the three months that she was in court, there were only three really good stories.

On the basis of the observations carried out in court, the presence of the press appeared to have little effect on proceedings. However, it was noticeable that, when identifying who was in the courtroom, magistrates were reluctant to identify the press to defendants and their families. In addition, defence and prosecution lawyers were reluctant to detail all the facts about the offender and offence if the press were in court. Although they made sure that the magistrates had all the facts they needed, if facts were available in a written form they referred to these documents rather than stating them in open court.

There was a press presence in two of the 39 case studies. In one case, in Rotherham, the defendant and his mother were happy about the press presence. The mother said that she felt all right because she knew that her son could not be named. In the other case, in Leicestershire, the defendant did not realise that the press were present during his case until after he left the courtroom. He said:

"I should have been told about that because I wouldn't have wanted them in."

In the remaining 37 cases defendants and their supporters were asked if they would have wanted the press to be in court. Twenty-nine of the defendants and 30 of their supporters said that they did not. While most defendants only said that the press being in court would make them feel uncomfortable, nervous or more careful about what they said, five said they would not have wanted to speak to the magistrates if the press had been in court, and two said that they would not have entered the courtroom. One defendant said that if the press had been in court she would not have paid attention to the magistrates because she would be trying to see what the press were writing. Parents tended to think that their children should be protected from the attention of the press: "...it's a child's court – it should be a closed court." Although it was not particularly apparent in the cases where the press attended court during the project, such reactions suggest that press presence could hinder engagement with defendants.

Key Youth Court personnel interviewed towards the end of the first phase of the project thought that the press had been in court more since the project started. Not surprisingly, this was especially evident at Leicester City Court where the press had attended for a trial period. Interviewees at the other courts felt that the press still only came to court if there was a "spicy" or "high profile" case. A clerk in Rotherham felt that, even if the press did not attend regularly, they were aware that they had a place in the courtroom, so that if there was a case they were interested in they remained in court longer rather than just scurrying in and out. In general, the increased press coverage in Leicester City Court was felt to have had a positive effect. A prosecution lawyer said the reports had raised public awareness in a good way. A concern expressed by a Youth Justice worker in Leicestershire was that there was a danger that an increase in stories about young offenders in the city newspaper as a result of the project might have made people think that youth offending had increased. Another Youth Justice worker, in Rotherham, thought the new layout might put reporters off if they felt the court was a tight circle that they were not a part of. Most of those completing the questionnaire sent to those who worked in the Youth Court towards the end of the first 12 months of the project said they thought there had been little change in attendance by members of the press since the Demonstration Project started. But this is not surprising, since there was still quite a high probability that any given magistrate, Youth Justice worker or solicitor would not be in court on a day when a reporter was present. Much the same picture emerged in responses to the follow-up questionnaire sent out in February 2000.

Lifting reporting restrictions

Neither area involved in the Demonstration Project had had any experience of reporting restrictions being lifted before the project started. In interviews at the start of the project, some caution was expressed about encouraging magistrates to consider lifting reporting restrictions in more cases, although it was acknowledged that it could be useful in certain instances as a way of warning the community about an offender. One of the main concerns was that naming offenders would give them status amongst their peers. It was also felt that there could be a danger of vendettas and vigilante attacks against offenders and their families. It was also thought that being 'named' could make it even harder for offenders to return to a normal life. The predominant view was that the child's welfare should be paramount when considering whether to lift reporting restrictions.

During the Demonstration Project there was one case in each court area where reporting restrictions were lifted. There were two further applications to lift reporting restrictions in Leicestershire, and one in Rotherham, that were turned down. Both areas included guidelines in their protocols on what magistrates should consider when deciding whether to grant an application to lift reporting restrictions.

In Leicester City Court (the court that had a specific initiative to involve the local press for a trial period), if the press wished to apply to have reporting restrictions lifted they notified the court in advance. Then on the day of the case itself they let the relevant court clerk know that they were going to make an application. Written arguments were also produced. After the magistrates heard the press application, other interested parties in court could also make applications to the magistrates. The magistrates then made a decision, with reference to the protocol. In Rotherham, although no similar system was put in place for dealing with applications to lift reporting restrictions, the protocol outlined the factors that should be considered when deciding whether to lift reporting restrictions. It also stated that prosecution and defence lawyers and court clerks should be allowed to make presentations about any application.

In Rotherham reporting restrictions were lifted in the case of a persistent young offender who received a custodial sentence early in 1999 for a number of vehicle offences, including driving dangerously and aggravated vehicle taking. The stipendiary magistrate took the view that it was a suitable case in which to lift reporting restrictions, but stood the case down to allow the defence solicitor to prepare objections. After hearing the presentation the stipendiary still thought the offender should be named. In Leicester City Court an offender found guilty of assault with a number of previous convictions was named in May 1999. The local newspaper made the application and the magistrates decided to name the offender after hearing representations from other interested parties.

In April 1999 the newspaper in Leicester reported that an application it had made to lift reporting restrictions had been turned down. This was the case of a 17-year-old 'persistent offender' sentenced to two years probation for 11 offences including theft, assault, criminal damage, arson and burglary. The magistrates refused to lift reporting restrictions after the defence solicitor stated that her client had suffered physical and emotional abuse and had special educational needs. The reporter involved said that if she had known about the offender's background she would not have made the application in the first place. In July 1999 the stipendiary magistrate in Leicester City Court refused to lift reporting restrictions in the case of a 16-year-old girl who had been convicted of assault occasioning actual bodily harm, aggravated burglary and intimidating a witness. His reasons were that the case was being sentenced in the Crown Court, and therefore the judge in that court should make the decision whether or not to name. In the meantime the public did not need to be warned about the girl because she was in custody. In the third case where an application was turned down, the stipendiary in Rotherham made the decision not to name the perpetrator of an assault. The local press made an application but the stipendiary did not grant it because he did not believe that the offender had acted maliciously, and his family had saved to provide compensation to the victim.

Thirty-four out of the 39 defendants involved in the case studies in the two areas said that they would not want their name to be in the papers; just five said that they would not have minded. One of the five said:

> "Everybody else in X and Y (the names of places) knows what I've done, so there'll be no difference there."

The main reason people did not want to be named was because they did not want their friends and family to know that they had been in court. There was also a feeling that the press might distort the facts. One defendant said that he would be worried that the press would make him out to be a thug. All the parents involved in the case studies said they would not want their children to be named in the press, and were worried about the effect of naming on their child's reputation. One mother said that her son already had a reputation for things that he had not done, and that if he were named more people would get the wrong idea. Another parent was worried about the effect that it would have on her son's job prospects. One mother said:

> "He's trying to make a fresh start, we're moving to a new home and he doesn't need that stigma."

A father had had the experience of being named himself:

> "I've had my name in the paper, so that is…terrible. Makes you think though, know what I mean?"

Three-quarters of the magistrates in the case studies said that they would not lift reporting restrictions in the current case. Eighteen per cent said that they would be prepared to consider lifting restrictions in the cases they were dealing with: three cases of theft and one each of criminal damage, intimidating a witness, nuisance and a public order offence. Two sets of magistrates said that they had not thought about lifting reporting restrictions. One of these magistrates said:

> "If a reporter was in court as a matter of course it would make you think 'this'd be one for the papers' … but because it's not something we're used to dealing with, there's nothing to remind us or make us … think that this is appropriate to lift it."

The main reason magistrates gave for not wishing to lift restrictions was that it was not in the public interest: "he's not upsetting the community by that action". The fact that a defendant was committing only their first or second offence was also a factor. Magistrates tended to say about these offenders that they were "not an out and out offender", "he's not a bad lad we're likely to see again", and "he's not really into crime is he?". Magistrates were also concerned about the adverse effect that naming could have on the defendant and his family. The fact that an offence was not very serious and the young age of the defendant were also given as reasons for not naming. One set of magistrates said that the public perception of the sentence concerned them:

> "It did go through my mind what the public perception of 18 months probation for burglary [would be]."

Magistrates who felt they could have named defendants in the case studies said that the age of the offender was an important consideration:

"At his age, I'm not sure whether reporting restrictions are actually appropriate, he's 18 in another three or four weeks, so personally it wouldn't have worried me if that appeared in the newspaper."

Other reasons to name defendants included having similar previous convictions, the fact that it would not harm the defendant to do so, and that it might act as a deterrent to others. The magistrates in these cases did not in fact lift reporting restrictions, and the non-presence of the press may have been a reason for not doing so.

Every defence solicitor interviewed said that they did not think it would be appropriate to lift reporting restrictions in their client's case. The most popular reasons were that naming was not right in principle for young people, that the offence was not serious enough to merit naming, and that it was not in the public interest to name the young person. Solicitors tended to feel that the privacy of a child should be preserved. There was also concern that naming would harm the defendant or their family, that the offence was a family matter; that the defendant was too young and that naming would not benefit the victim.

One of the case studies received considerable publicity and is worth describing in more detail. X was named by the Leicester newspaper in May 1999. He was 16 years old when sentenced for three assaults occasioning actual bodily harm. He had attacked two elderly gentlemen, for which he received two three-month concurrent terms in a Young Offender Institution, and a 17-year-old girl for which he received another consecutive two-month term. He had a number of previous convictions and was at the time of his sentence already serving time in a Young Offender Institution for an aggravated TWOC (taking a vehicle without owner's consent). In the past he had received two attendance centre orders and a supervision order. His past offences included threatening behaviour, assault and affray. X himself made no comment about the decision to lift reporting restrictions, but his mother was upset and angry about it. She believed her family would be under threat of retaliation if her son's name was in the paper, and said the family had already had three bricks through their windows.

The reasons given by the magistrates for deciding to name X were that:

- they felt his offending was serious and persistent and had an impact on people in his locality

- they did not think that the publicity would lead to him or his family being harassed

- they did not believe that X was too young or vulnerable to be named

- they did not feel that he was contrite or had taken responsibility for what he had done, and had made his victims go through the trauma of a trial

- they did not think that his name being in the paper would prejudice magistrates that may hear the case on appeal.

The magistrates felt they had had ample guidance from the legal advisor and other parties in court to make their decision, and had referred to the Home Office Circular issued in conjunction with the Demonstration Project to check whether the case matched the criteria set.

X's solicitor complained about the lack of notice he had been given about the application to lift reporting restrictions, and said that he had not been given access to any criteria for lifting reporting restrictions. He was unaware that he could have asked the bench for time to prepare his objection to the application. The news story appeared on the front page of the city newspaper alongside an editorial that explained its reasons for requesting restrictions to be lifted. The main reason was that it was felt to be in the public interest, although it was acknowledged that it could reinforce an offender's alienation from society. A further article appeared in the newspaper, which reported the support for this decision from Leicestershire's Police Federation and the Chairman of Leicester City Court's Youth Court Panel. Two letters appeared in the newspaper about the decision, one in favour and the other against.

Since reporting restrictions had been lifted only once in each court area during the period of the Demonstration Project, not many people involved in the work of the Youth Court had direct experience of it. So most of those commenting on the issue towards the end of the first phase of the project did so in general terms, and not surprisingly views had changed little since the start of the project. One probation officer in Leicestershire was concerned that she had not been made aware of the criteria under which applications could be made, and felt that there was no evidence to show that naming offenders reduced re-offending. She also believed that naming could further alienate young people from society and lead to their families being victimised. This view was mirrored by a Youth Justice worker in Rotherham who said that the children named would be most likely to come from problem families, who might then be victimised. Youth Justice workers were particularly likely to say that they would like to see the idea of lifting reporting restrictions dropped. In the questionnaire sent to all those involved in the work of the Youth Court towards the end of the first phase of the project, respondents were asked whether they were in favour of the lifting of reporting restrictions in certain cases. Seven out of ten of all respondents (73%) said they were, but when magistrates alone are considered this rose to more than eight out of ten (84%).

The majority of people who completed the follow-up questionnaire (approximately two-thirds in Rotherham and almost six out of ten in Leicestershire, omitting 'can't says') said that their views on lifting reporting restrictions had not changed since the project started. A quarter of respondents in Rotherham and four out of ten in Leicestershire said that they had become more in favour of lifting reporting restrictions since the project started. Eighteen per cent in Rotherham and 35 per cent in Leicestershire said that they had become more in favour within the six months prior to receiving the follow-up questionnaire. Very few in each area (three or four people) had become less favourable, although in both areas it was the magistrates who had become more favourable towards lifting reporting restrictions than the other groups involved with the Youth Court. Respondents were asked whether they thought any lifting of reporting restrictions had been beneficial, adverse or had little impact. Amongst those who felt they were able to express a view, seven out of ten people (72%) in Rotherham and almost as many (68%) in Leicestershire said they thought that there had been little impact. Fourteen per cent in Rotherham and 23 per cent in Leicestershire said they thought the impact had been beneficial, with twice as many magistrates inclined to this view in Leicestershire as other professions.

Attendance by other parties

The law permits attendance in the Youth Court by members and officers of the court, parties to the case, and representatives of news agencies, and by 'such persons as the court may specially authorise to be present' (Children and Young Persons Act 1933, s. 47 (2)(d)). The topic of who may be permitted to be present in the Youth Court was discussed in the early stages of the project. Concerns focused on the need to protect young people, whether present as defendants or in some other capacity, from undue attention, and on the practical matter of limited space which some of the new layouts diminished further. However, it was said in both areas that people with a legitimate interest should be permitted in court (and this was written into the protocol for Rotherham). This might include a defendant's schoolteacher, religious adviser, close friend of the family, or some other person concerned with a child's welfare. As ever, the final decision would be with the magistrates in a given case. Teachers and youth workers were occasionally seen in court in support of young defendants during the observations for the Demonstration Project, but members of the public did not attend.

Evaluating attendance by victims and the press

Many of those involved with the Youth Court supported the idea of opening up the Youth Court and making it more accessible to victims and the press, although not the public in general, and efforts were made to encourage attendance. However, there were concerns about the practical difficulties that could be involved, and the possibility of unwanted consequences resulting from victim and press attendance.

As far as victims were concerned, one problem was whether the police could name defendants in letters to victims so that they could find the courtrooms where their cases were being heard more easily. Rotherham and Leicester City Court had adequate facilities and Victim and Witness Support workers who were prepared to look after victims attending court, but this was not true in all courts. There was also concern that changes to court layout might affect victims' experiences of court because of the lack of space and proximity to the defendant, and that the presence of a victim might inhibit productive engagement with the offender. If victims are to be given encouragement to attend Youth Court hearings then clearly more attention needs to be devoted to overcoming the practical obstacles. This research is not alone in drawing attention to the need for further work in this area. In 1998 a study of witness care in magistrates' courts and the Youth Court said,

> 'Non-separation of defence and prosecution witnesses and inadequate security, **especially in the Youth Court**, increased intimidation risks for prosecution witnesses' (Plotnikoff and Woolfson, 1998. Emphasis added).

On the other hand, the lack of victim presence in the adult court and the small number of witnesses in trials who chose to remain in court after giving evidence suggested that victims might simply not want to attend the Youth Court. If this is the case then it may be important to concentrate on making sure that victims have adequate information about the outcome of their case, and a clear understanding of what sentences involve.

Although Leicester City Court had some success in encouraging the press to attend the Youth Court more for a time, it appears that in general newspapers wish to be selective in their attendance at, and reporting of, what happens there. It may be, therefore, that the best option for Youth Courts is to develop good contacts with their local media (local radio stations might be included) with a view to encouraging better public awareness of youth justice issues in general.

Magistrates only considered lifting restrictions in a few cases, possibly because of the lack of a press presence in the courtroom, and restrictions were only lifted once in each area. Although magistrates were glad to have the option of lifting reporting restrictions available, the indications were that they would use it infrequently because naming an offender could have drawbacks as well as advantages. Youth Justice workers, defence solicitors and the families of defendants were most likely to express concern about the lifting of reporting restrictions. Existing advice about what factors should be considered by magistrates when deciding whether to lift reporting restrictions appeared to be adequate, but it may be that clerks need to remind magistrates of their powers from time to time. In cases where applications to lift reporting restrictions were made by the press, the clear message was that all parties involved in the case needed to know full details of the application as soon as possible.

In England and Wales most information relating to criminal justice matters has been produced centrally by the Home Office or the Lord Chancellor's Department, and covers such matters as sentencing and the time taken to deal with cases. Although this information is provided by local agencies such as the police and courts, it has not generally been circulated to courts and other criminal justice personnel on a disaggregated basis so that they can consider what has been happening in their area. Even where such information is available it is rare for Youth Court information to be produced on a separate basis. Around the country individual courts may keep their own statistics about court proceedings, and some of these are published in Annual Reports. But the form that these take varies widely. Most commonly courts will record and circulate information regarding workloads and other administrative matters. However, the telephone survey of ten other courts taken in connection with the evaluation of the Demonstration Project revealed that at least two courts regularly circulated information to its Youth Court Panel and User Group about such matters as bail, sentencing and breaches.

In initial interviews, personnel in both Demonstration Project areas said they thought there was a lack of useful feedback information about sentences. In Rotherham the manager of the local Youth Justice team had produced information about sentences from time to time at Youth Court User Group meetings (which do not ordinarily involve many magistrates). This was done on a voluntary basis, using records kept by the team on a rather old-fashioned database, and involved a special effort on her part to compile the information. Magistrates in Leicestershire said that in the main such feedback as they received about their work came about as a result of breach proceedings, appeals and the return of young offenders who committed further offences. Leicestershire magistrates also occasionally found out whether a community service order was completed. There was some concern amongst interviewees that if feedback on sentencing patterns were to be produced more regularly, then it should not affect the way future cases were dealt with. In general magistrates wanted information about overall trends and patterns rather than feedback on individual cases, although it was felt that there were occasions when this might be appropriate. This is consistent with the findings of another demonstration project that aimed to increase sentencers' confidence in community sentences, which suggested that sentencers were only interested in receiving information regarding a few individuals where they were especially concerned about offenders' progress (Hedderman, Ellis and Sugg, 1999: ix). Youth Justice workers felt that it was important that any feedback should occur in meetings where it would be possible to explain what the information meant and discuss its implications. While it was felt to be most appropriate for the Youth Justice Team (soon to become a Youth

Offending Team as a result of the Crime and Disorder Act 1998) to produce feedback information, it was pointed out that this would make demands on their time and resources.

It was decided by both areas taking part in the Demonstration Project that the most appropriate way to provide court users with feedback about court decisions was by producing a newsletter. An example of the newsletters produced is included in Appendix E. In Rotherham the manager of the local Youth Justice team liaised with the Home Office to produce a sentencing newsletter that was distributed to magistrates in April 1999. Leicestershire decided that providing feedback needed to be produced on a countywide basis, and a newsletter was produced with the help of the Home Office and distributed in April 1999, together with a questionnaire to magistrates to assess their views of this feedback. A second newsletter was produced and distributed in Leicestershire in March 2000.

In the interviews that took place in the summer of 1999, those who had seen them universally praised the newsletters. There were, however, a number of suggestions about how they could be improved, including more local information, presenting the information in a simpler form, and the inclusion of some explanation of the facts and figures.

In the questionnaire respondents were asked about the kinds of information that they would find it most helpful to know regarding the work of the court, rating various items 'not particularly' (scoring 1 point), 'possibly' (2 points), 'probably' (3 points) and 'definitely' (scoring 4 points). The mean scores and rankings for the various items are given in Table 6.1.

Table 6.1:   Ratings for feedback information wanted

Information about:	All respondents		Magistrates only	
	mean score	ranking	mean score	ranking
Reconviction rates	3.33	1	3.59	1
Breaches of court orders	3.16	2	3.39	2
Completion rates of sentences	3.12	3	3.37	3
Sentencing patterns	3.08	4	3.05	5
Progress of certain individuals	2.80	5	3.15	4
Content of specific sentences	2.75	6	2.92	6
Number of pre-sentence reports requested or prepared	2.19	7	2.16	7

Reconviction rates stand out as the information that magistrates and others would most like to know about. This was also apparent from the fact that 63 per cent of all respondents and 74 per cent of magistrates said that this was information that they would 'definitely' like to know. It was also the matter mentioned most often in discussions in meetings, where it was recognised that this was also the most problematic information to produce and make use of. This is partly because of the need to conduct follow-up studies, and also because of the problem of interpreting such information, since reconviction rates are susceptible to the influence of a range of factors apart from court decisions.

Asked how often they would like to have such feedback the most popular interval was quarterly, with 45 per cent of all respondents and 49 per cent of magistrates indicating this option. Around a quarter of people (24% of all respondents and 28% of magistrates) said they would wish to have such feedback on a six monthly basis, and about one in ten respondents said they would like it to be annual, with rather more than another one in ten saying they would like it monthly. Respondents were also asked how they would like the information to be provided. Some seven out of ten of all respondents (73%) said they would like it in a newsletter. This was even more popular with magistrates with eight out of ten (81%) indicating this option. Almost half the magistrates (45%) said they would wish to have the information available at a Youth Court Panel meeting but, not surprisingly, other court users were more likely to indicate that they would like it to be available at a Youth Court User Group meeting. Respondents could tick more than one of the options offered, and the pattern of responses was such as to suggest that what respondents were saying was that they wanted the information to be available initially in a newsletter, but also wanted the opportunity to discuss it in whichever forum was the most appropriate for them, either a Panel meeting or a User Group meeting.

In response to the follow-up questionnaire those who had seen such a feedback newsletter overwhelmingly said they found it useful (94% in Rotherham and 98% in Leicestershire), and irrespective of whether or not they had seen such a report at any time, eight out of every ten respondents said they would like to have this kind of information. The majority of respondents in both areas said they thought the provision of feedback had been beneficial. However, although all magistrates were sent a copy of the newsletter in Rotherham just over half of magistrates and four out of ten other people involved in the work of the Youth Court recalled seeing a report on the sentencing decisions of the court during the initial evaluation period. In Leicestershire just 44 per cent of magistrates and 23 per cent of others said that they had seen such a report.

The newsletters provided by the two court areas have been a successful development, and magistrates have been happy with the provision of general statistics on sentencing. However, it should be noted that the Home Office Research, Development and Statistics Directorate played an important role in producing the newsletters, which is something that may be more difficult in the future. Individual courts might need to consider working in collaboration with the Home Office and their Youth Offending Team regarding the provision of similar information in the future.

7   Other aspects of the project

Sentencing

Although a stronger emphasis on using sentencing to prevent future offending was a formal aim of the Demonstration Project, relatively few of the participants saw changing the way that young offenders were sentenced as an objective (see Chapter 2). It is nonetheless of some interest to know whether the project did have an impact on the way in which young people were sentenced. The questionnaire asked people whether they thought this had happened at all, and three out of ten magistrates (32%) said that they had changed their minds about what sentence to give as a result of the changes initiated by the Demonstration Project. In the interviews and informal discussion it was explained that this was usually because, as a result of engaging with defendants and their supporters more, they had become aware of matters that previously they would not have found out about.

Information on sentencing in the two court areas was provided by the Home Office for the three quarter years prior to the start of the Demonstration Project (that is, the first three quarters, Q1 to Q3, of 1998) and the three quarters after the project started (Q4, 1998 – Q2, 1999). Thus it is possible to make a comparison between the nine months before and the nine months after the project started. However, it could be argued that the last quarter of 1998 (1998, Q4) is not a good comparison, since the project was only in the early stages of development. The information has therefore been analysed not only for the three quarters Q4, 1998 to Q2, 1999 combined, but also for the three quarters separately. Care needs to be taken when interpreting the data, since some of the numbers involved are quite small and can yield somewhat misleading percentage changes. The number and proportion of cases committed to the Crown Court for sentence is also reported, since the extent of committal for sentence can affect the pattern of sentencing at the magistrates' court itself. The data for 1999 were provisional when supplied. The data relevant to the Youth Courts were extracted from a spreadsheet supplied by the Home Office.

The tables presented here are derived from these more detailed tables, and focus on sentencing patterns. Any changes in sentencing patterns may, of course, reflect changes in patterns of offending dealt with by the courts, which has been taken into consideration. Table 7.1 summarises the pattern of sentencing for Rotherham Youth Court for the nine months before and after the start of the Demonstration Project, and for the separate quarters after the project started.

Table 7.1: **Rotherham – Summary of sentencing, quarter 1 1998 – quarter 2 1999 (percentage)**

	Q1 1998 – Q3 1998	Q4 1998 – Q2 1999	Q4 1998	Q1 1999	Q2 1999
Committed for sentence	1	1	1	1	–
Discharge	29	42	42	40	45
Fine	14	9	9	10	3
Probation order	2	5	7	5	6
Supervision order	17	11	15	10	3
Community service order	7	7	3	11	6
Attendance centre order	15	16	12	16	23
Combination order	3	2	4	1	–
Young offenders institute	11	6	6	7	6
Otherwise dealt with	1	2	1	–	6
Total number	295	221	88	103	36

Note: Columns may not add up to 100% because of rounding.
Calculations for 1999 were based on provisional figures.

It is worth noting that the most common offence for both 10- to 13 and 14- to 17-year-olds was theft and handling, followed for 14- to 17-year-olds by summary non-motoring offences. The pattern of offences did not change much between the periods before and after the start of the Demonstration Project.

There were statistically significant changes in sentencing for the nine months following the start of the Demonstration Project (Q4, 1998 – Q2, 1999), compared with the nine months preceding it (Q1 – Q3, 1998) as shown in Table 7.2.

Table 7.2: **Rotherham – Changes in sentencing**

Sentence	Change	t statistic	probability level
Absolute and Conditional Discharges	Increased	3.27	.01
Probation Orders	Increased	2.8	.01
Fines	Decreased	2.22	.05
Supervision Orders	Decreased	2.07	.05
Young Offender Institution	Decreased	2.11	.05

Note: The t-tests were conducted on the proportions sentenced in the magistrates' courts excluding those committed for sentence.

There were no statistically significant changes in the other disposals. It may also be noted that when the three quarters following the start of the project are looked at separately, the last quarter of 1998 is more like the quarters that followed it than those which preceded it. This suggests that, if the changes in sentencing patterns are related to the Demonstration Project, then it was the inception of the project itself, as much as the introduction of any particular measure, which had an impact. However, it must also be noted that the changes in sentencing observed could be due to a variety of other causes.

Although there were some small variations, the same shift in the pattern of sentencing was not so apparent at the Leicestershire courts, as shown by Table 7.3.

Table 7.3:   *All Leicestershire courts - Summary of sentencing, quarter 1 1998 – quarter 2 1999 (percentage)*

	Q1 1998 – Q3 1998	Q4 1998 – Q2 1999	Q4 1998	Q1 1999	Q2 1999
Committed for sentence	7	6	9	6	5
Discharge	19	21	21	22	20
Fine	13	16	15	12	20
Probation order	4	5	4	7	5
Supervision order	15	13	13	15	12
Community service order	7	7	9	8	5
Attendance centre order	20	16	16	13	18
Combination order	3	4	4	3	4
Young offenders institute	9	8	6	8	9
Otherwise dealt with	3	4	3	5	3
Total number	961	849	287	280	282

Note: Columns may not add up to 100% because of rounding.

Only attendance centre orders showed any statistically significant change ($t = 2.72$, $p < .01$), decreasing by five per cent during the nine months following the start of the Demonstration Project compared with the nine months preceding it. It is possible that differences may have occurred at individual courts within Leicestershire, but the numbers involved at this level of disaggregation are not susceptible to detecting changes that may be due to any impact that the project may have had.

Overall opinions of the project

The final question that people were asked in the questionnaires circulated in mid-1999 (nine months into the project) and in February 2000 (another nine months later) was whether they thought the Demonstration Project had been beneficial, adverse or had had little impact. The response to this question changed somewhat between the two periods as Table 7.4 shows.

Table 7.4:   Impact of the project

	First Survey		Follow-Up Survey	
	Number	Percentage[1]	Number	Percentage[1]
Beneficial	67	31	96	56
Little impact	120	56	63	37
Adverse	26	11	13	7
Can't say	34	–	19	–
Total number	247	100	191	100

Note:
1.   Percentage omits the 'Can't says'.

After the first nine months of the project more than half of the respondents felt that the project had made little impact, whereas nine months later a much smaller proportion thought this. Of those who felt able to express an opinion and who thought the project had had an impact, the majority thought the impact had been beneficial. This suggests that it is important to give new developments in the Youth Court sufficient time to become recognised and accepted.

There were some differences between the two areas, with those in Rotherham being more likely to see the project as having had a beneficial impact. In the first survey more than half (54%) of Rotherham magistrates said they thought the impact of the project had been beneficial, whereas in Leicestershire only 28 per cent did so. In the follow-up survey three-quarters of the magistrates and six out of ten of all others in Rotherham (omitting 'can't says') said they thought the project had had a beneficial effect. In Leicestershire 49 per cent of the magistrates and 51 per cent of others said they thought the Demonstration Project had had an overall beneficial impact.

Financial implications

The financial implications of the Demonstration Project were also recorded. None of the courts had to put on extra courts or hire extra staff as a result of the project, so the costs were limited to the training days, and the cost of producing the sentencing newsletters. In Rotherham it was calculated that the cost to the court of the Demonstration Project was £2,800. In addition, the newsletter was co-produced by the local Youth Justice manager. Her time was costed at £240. In Leicestershire the cost of the project to the courts was £2,397.07. Home Office researchers produced their newsletters. They had also helped in the production of the newsletter in Rotherham, and in total, the contributions cost £2,640. The Home Office incurred costs as it held a seminar in London for the two court areas taking part in the project, but these have not been included as they would not be relevant to other courts that might wish to implement the measures examined in the Demonstration Project.

The follow-up period

The first phase of the research drew to a close in September 1999. This was followed by another period of fieldwork lasting from mid-February to the end of March 2000. Understandably the early stages of a new development are characterised by change and uncertainty, and a lot of attention is focused on a new project. The intention of a follow-up six months after the first phase was to see how the changes brought about as a result of the Demonstration Project were faring having been left in operation for a while, and when the people involved had had an opportunity to acclimatise to them. With some exceptions (such as further guidance being given on engagement in Rotherham), there was little new development during the six months between the first phase of the research and the follow-up period. Those interviewed during the follow-up period said that the previous six months had been a period of settling in rather than a time in which new developments had occurred. This was seen as positive by many interviewees, who felt that it had allowed the project to become part of the running of the court and for people at court to get used to it. The project was described as "running smoother now" and "a reinforcement of what has gone before". A magistrate in Leicestershire said that the Demonstration Project had been accepted as the 'status quo', and it had helped people to realise that the Youth Court could and would evolve. A court clerk in Rotherham said that there had been a "learning curve in the first six months", but the project had now settled down to be the norm. He thought the extension of the project from October 1999 to March 2000 had been good, since the project had continued without any further input being needed. However, a few interviewees felt that the project may have lost some of its initial impetus. Twelve of the 28 people interviewed said they felt more positive about the Demonstration Project since its extension, and a further ten said that their initial opinion (usually a positive one) had not changed. Engagement by magistrates with defendants, and the fact that the project had settled down were cited as the most popular reasons to feel positive about the project. Only two interviewees (one from each court area) said that they felt more negative about the project since the extension. When asked how they thought their colleagues felt about the project, ten interviewees who expressed an opinion said that their colleagues were more positive now than six months ago, one said that they were more negative, and five said their colleagues' opinions had not changed. Again the most popular reason for a positive answer was that their colleagues had got more used to the project.

8 Other developments in youth justice

At the time the Demonstration Project was in progress, several other developments in youth justice were taking place that are worth mentioning because they had a bearing on changes introduced by the Demonstration Project. One such development was the fact that courts throughout the country were implementing measures designed to reduce delay in dealing with cases. In particular Youth Courts were expected to 'fast track' persistent young offenders, and from October 1998 the time taken to deal with such offenders was being monitored (for further details on the measures and effectiveness of fast tracking see Crow and Stubbing, 2000). Reference has already been made in Chapter 3 to the need to deal with cases as speedily as possible, where it was reported that engagement between magistrates and offenders and their families did not appear to have any effect on the length of hearings. However, some of those interviewed during the course of the project said they thought that fast tracking had meant that there was little if any opportunity to inform victims about a case.

The Crime and Disorder Act 1998 provided for a number of new orders which courts could use in dealing with young offenders, and for the setting up of Youth Offending Teams (YOTs). At the time the Demonstration Project was taking place these measures were being piloted in certain areas, but not in the areas involved in the Demonstration Project. However, it was anticipated that the provisions of the 1998 Act would soon be implemented throughout the country, and therefore the courts taking part in the project had at least half an eye on how the changes introduced as part of the Demonstration Project might work alongside the new provisions. One positive likelihood was that the new Youth Offending Team would in future have more up-to-date information available about young offenders dealt with by the court which could be fed back to sentencers, for example in a newsletter such as that produced during the course of the Demonstration Project. A court clerk in Rotherham said that the feedback had been good: "short, snappy and to the point". But he thought that people did not just want to know the number of orders that had been made; they wanted to know about their effectiveness, and this would be more relevant with the Crime and Disorder Act.

Thirteen of the 28 people who took part in follow-up interviews thought that increased engagement between magistrates and defendants and their parents would help in deciding how best to use the new orders so that they would be appropriately targeted and directed at stopping offending. A youth justice worker considered that engagement would become doubly important because magistrates would have to explain to parents why they expected them to comply with an order, and this could help to ensure that parents completed orders. Three interviewees mentioned that the work to encourage victim attendance in the Youth Court might be more relevant with the introduction of reparation orders and the responsibility of the Youth Offending Teams to consult with victims.

Another important issue for the future arising out of the Demonstration Project concerns the effect on the Youth Court of the Youth Justice and Criminal Evidence Act 1999. Under this Act, young offenders who appear in the Youth Court for the first time and plead guilty will normally be referred by the court to a youth offender panel (unless the court wishes to pass a custodial sentence, a hospital order or an absolute discharge). There have been some suggestions that the changes involved in the Demonstration Project are more suitable for less experienced and younger offenders, who may be more amenable to a less formal approach. Some of those involved in the project felt that older and more experienced offenders are both more difficult to engage with, and more likely to treat attempts at openness and informality with contempt, with deleterious effects on the dignity of the court. This raises the possibility that the younger offenders and those with least criminal history for whom the changes in the Youth Court might work best are the ones most likely to be referred to the Youth Offender Panel. If this is the case, it might be that the changes introduced by the Demonstration Project become less easy to apply to the Youth Court, and that engagement in a less formal setting will be experienced by young offenders when they appear before a Youth Offender Panel in future, rather than in the setting of the Youth Court.

This was discussed at a meeting of senior personnel and users from both court areas to review the Demonstration Project in July 1999. The result of this discussion was to conclude that the changes introduced by the Demonstration Project would still be relevant to Youth Courts in the future, despite the changes in prospect as a result of the Youth Justice and Criminal Evidence Act 1999. Although it was recognised that some magistrates might feel there was less point in trying to engage with more persistent offenders, those taking part in the discussion felt that greater engagement with all types of young defendant was not only possible, but had been achieved during the course of the project. Indeed one view was that the project was more relevant to, and effective with, older and more persistent offenders. Deferred sentences in particular had been used to good effect with such defendants in conjunction with attempts to engage with them about their offending behaviour.

An important development in the way that young offenders are dealt with in court occurred in February 2000. As a result of a ruling of the European Court of Human Rights in *T v UK* and *V v UK*[3] the Lord Chief Justice issued a Practice Direction[4]. The Practice Direction has been referred to already in relevant parts of this report. Although it is directed at the Crown Court, some of its paragraphs relate directly to measures implemented as a result of the Demonstration Project. Of particular relevance are the following paragraphs:

Paragraph 3 says that, 'All possible steps should be taken to assist the young defendant to understand and participate in the proceedings',

Paragraph 6 says that 'It might be appropriate to arrange that a young defendant should visit, out of court hours and before the trial, the courtroom in which the trial was to be held so that he could familiarise himself with it',

Paragraph 9 says, 'The trial should, if practicable, be held in a courtroom in which all the participants are on the same level or almost the same level',

Paragraph 10 says, 'A young defendant should normally, if he wishes, be free to sit with members of his family or others in a place which permit easy, informal communication with his legal representatives and others with whom he wants or needs to communicate',

Paragraph 11 says, 'The court should explain the course of proceedings to a young defendant in terms he could understand, should remind those representing a young defendant of their continuing duty to explain each step of the trial to him and should ensure, so far as practicable, that the trial is conducted in language which the young defendant could understand',

Paragraph 13 says, 'Any person responsible for the security of a young defendant who is in custody should not be in uniform. There should be no recognisable police presence in the courtroom save for good reason',

Paragraph 14 says, 'The court should be prepared to restrict attendance at the trial to a small number, perhaps limited to some of those with an immediate and direct interest in the outcome of the trial'.

While most of the paragraphs cited above are in line with the changes made during the Demonstration Project, the last mentioned is at some variance with the attempts made by the

---

3   Applications 24274/96 and 24888/96 (1999) and Criminal Law Review, (2000), 187.
4   [2000] 2 All ER 285.

project to encourage wider attendance, but the matter of attendance is at the discretion of the court. The practice direction was discussed in meetings that took place in the courts involved in the project, and by those interviewed during the follow-up period. The view of those concerned was that the changes in court layout and procedure that had taken place as a part of the Demonstration Project were now the way forward for the Youth Court, and the practice direction reinforced what the project had set out to achieve.

During the course of the Demonstration Project there was an awareness by some project participants that the Human Rights Act 1998 might also have implications for the Youth Court when implemented on 2 October 2000. But these implications were still under consideration at the time the project was taking place, and there was no significant discussion about their relevance to the measures adopted as part of the Demonstration Project.

Having examined the various initiatives implemented as part of the Demonstration Project, did the project indeed make progress towards achieving the aims of engaging young offenders and their parents in focusing on offending behaviour, creating a Youth Court which is more open and commands the confidence of victims and the public, and placing a stronger emphasis on using sentencing to prevent future offending? In answering this question it should be recalled that at the start of the project the courts involved were encouraged to try things out, and to find what worked best in the circumstances in which they found themselves. It was not expected that everything would work first time, and indeed adjustments were made during the course of the project.

As far as engaging defendants and their parents is concerned, the project succeeded in demonstrating that direct communication between magistrates and young offenders was a welcome and viable development, and that on the whole the young offenders themselves responded well to it. In the early stages of a case magistrates can introduce themselves and others and ensure that all concerned understand what is happening. At the sentencing stage magistrates can engage more directly with young offenders in addressing their offending behaviour, and this may assist them in arriving at the most suitable sentence. It is obviously important that magistrates do not make inappropriate interventions, and some magistrates were apprehensive about this at first. But clear guidelines and training can be effective in giving magistrates the confidence to know when to intervene and when not to. The experience of the Demonstration Project showed that training was an important part of encouraging engagement, and courts may well be able to exchange experiences, leading to the promotion of best practice. The other consideration as far as this part of the Demonstration Project is concerned is the need to emphasise the importance of parental attendance at the sentencing stage.

Creating a Youth Court that is more open and commands the confidence of victims and the public is more problematic, since much depends on factors outside the control of the court itself, such as the inclination of victims and the involvement of the press. There are also important practical and ethical considerations. Despite the fact that victim and press attendance was infrequent and unpredictable, the courts involved in the project showed that victims, the press and appropriate members of the public could be catered for and made to feel that the Youth Court was responsive to them. It is also worth noting that a more open Youth Court that commands greater public confidence does not necessarily need to have victims, press and public frequently present. What matters as much as anything is the development of an open and responsive environment, where the community and its representatives do not feel excluded, and that what goes on in the Youth Court is no concern of theirs.

The layout of the court is an important factor both in creating such an open and responsive atmosphere, and in facilitating engagement. Those who took part in the Demonstration Project had various concerns about changing the physical layout of the courtroom, in part because they did not want to create a setting which undermined the status and significance of a court appearance, but also because there were real practical considerations about ensuring that all those involved felt as comfortable as possible, and did not feel intimidated or threatened. The movement of the magistrates from a raised bench to the well of the court was a particular source of concern to some, but many came to accept the change, if not immediately, then after they had had the opportunity to become used to it for a while. This is particularly important in the light of a recent Practice Direction of the Lord Chief Justice, following the Thompson and Venables case, that when children are tried in the Crown Court all participants should normally sit on the same level (see Chapter 8).

Placing more emphasis on using sentencing to prevent future offending was an aim which was addressed more indirectly than directly during the course of the Demonstration Project. It was certainly an aspect of engaging with young offenders, and many magistrates said they felt they were sentencing with more confidence that their decisions were the right ones. It is significant that in Rotherham at least there appeared to have been a change in sentencing patterns associated with (if not necessarily a direct consequence of) the project.

Apart from the specific developments that comprised the Demonstration Project, did the project as a whole have a significant impact on the courts involved? For a while many of those who worked at the courts felt that it did not. One of the lessons of the project is that it can take some time for changes to be successfully implemented and become accepted as part of the normal working practice of the court. Several aspects of the project were only beginning to have an impact by the end of the first year. Extending the project to allow for a follow-up period was important, since this allowed time for new practices to be 'fine tuned' and to become less unusual and more acceptable. By the time of the follow-up study most of those who thought the project had made an impact said that it was for the better.

Throughout this report the results of the project have been reported with reference to two court areas. The reasons for involving two areas were to ensure that the results of any changes were not just the result of a one-off fluke and, more importantly, to be able to learn lessons from implementing the project in two different settings. Although the two areas acted independently, they were encouraged to discuss their experiences with each other and, apart from informal contacts, two formal meetings took place in February and July 1999. A distinctive feature of the project was that one of the courts, Leicester City, was a large inner city court, and it may be easier for such a court to try things out than smaller courts. This is partly a matter of resources, but also because changes may be more easily accommodated within the ethos of a larger court. On the other hand smaller courts may be able to more easily organise for change. Another feature of the project was the contrast between a single court in a medium sized town (Rotherham) and a large county with several court locations (Leicestershire). It was much easier for Rotherham to have direct contact with everyone involved and to implement changes more rapidly, whereas Leicestershire needed to set up a more extensive structure of consultation and decision making. This means that when changes are initiated, allowance may need to be made for the fact that courts may implement them in different ways and at different rates.

One feature of the Youth Court which was frequently discussed during the course of the project was the fact that the Youth Court has to deal with a wide variety of young people, from children who may be as young as ten and appearing for the first time in a strange and frightening situation, to youths who are close to adulthood and for whom the Youth Court may be all too familiar territory. Indeed on several occasions in the early months of the project it was suggested that there might need to be two kinds of Youth Court to take account of the varying age and experience of young offenders. As the project progressed this was mentioned less often, partly as a result of the impending implications of the Youth Justice and Criminal Evidence Act 1999 (see below), but it served to illustrate that dealing with such a variety of circumstances requires sensitivity and flexibility. To impose a set way of doing things would defeat the purpose of decreasing exclusivity and making Youth Courts more open, inclusive and able to deal with the wide variety of circumstances that lie behind offending behaviour.

Although it is important to assess the project as a whole, there was the potential for some aspects of the Demonstration Project to conflict with others to a certain extent. On the one hand, the intention was to open up the 'secret garden' of the Youth Court by encouraging greater attendance by victims, press and members of the public and lifting reporting restrictions more often. On the other hand, the aim was also to create a less formal atmosphere in order to foster communication between magistrates, defendants and parents. Arguably, the more the court is opened up, the more people there are in limited space, and the more participants are aware that proceedings will be known and reported to others, the less likely participants are to feel able to engage in frank discussion. Paragraph 14 of the practice direction quoted in the previous chapter indicates that in the Crown Court attendance should be restricted to those with an immediate and direct interest in the case, and this would settle such concerns. In the Demonstration Project courts the changes aimed at creating more dialogue between magistrates and offenders have generally made more progress and been more welcomed than those involving victims, the press and public. It may be that this is because engagement is something more directly under the control of the court itself, but it also means that the problem of arriving at a balance between successful engagement and opening up the Youth Court remains to be resolved.

Appendix A   The research

The research involved:

i) Attendance at key meetings

Thirty-six meetings were attended altogether in both court areas. These included:

- 8 project Board meetings in Leicestershire

- 1 Steering Group meeting in Rotherham

- 14 Panel and User Group meetings at all benches

- 13 miscellaneous meetings, including project launches, training sessions and joint meetings of representatives of the two court areas taking part in the project.

ii) Interviews with key personnel at three stages of the project;

Interviews were conducted with 26 people involved in the Youth Courts in Rotherham and Leicestershire to gain detailed accounts of how representatives from a number of agencies (magistrates, court clerks/legal advisors, defence and prosecution lawyers and Youth Justice and Probation workers) viewed the Demonstration Project, both before it established itself in the court, and after it had been in place for six months. Initial interviews took place between October and December 1998, and the later interviews took place between May and July 1999. As far as possible the same people were interviewed. However, there were a small number of differences due to interviewees moving out of the area or having had little experience of the project. During the follow-up period 28 people were interviewed. This involved, as far as possible, the same people as previously, plus one representative of victim support services in each area.

iii) Observations in court

Observations were made at all the courts taking part in the Demonstration Project. This involved 110 sessions in Rotherham, 78 sessions in Leicester City court, 10 in Market Bosworth court, 7 in Ashby de la Zouch, 9 in Loughborough court and 3 sessions at Melton Mowbray court during the course of the research. Further details of the court observations are included in Appendix B.

iv) A questionnaire to all personnel involved with the Youth Court

A questionnaire was distributed to 452 people involved with the Youth Court towards the end of the first year of the research. A total of 246 completed questionnaires were returned, giving a response rate of 54 per cent. A further questionnaire was distributed during the follow-up period. A total of 194 completed follow-up questionnaires were analysed, a response rate of 51 per cent. Further details and the results from each questionnaire can be found in Appendices C and D.

v) A small number of detailed case studies, including interviews with the parties involved in each case

Forty case studies were undertaken during the year to analyse in more detail how the project affected individual cases. Twenty were conducted in each court area. Details of these case studies are included in Appendix C. Case studies were conducted after observing a case to sentencing. Afterwards, offenders and their supporters, if in court, were interviewed, as were the magistrates who sat on the case. Defence solicitors were interviewed where possible for an additional perspective. Throughout this report sections referring to case studies are based on 39 of the 40 case studies. This is because one case study involved an offender in Leicestershire who was named in the local newspaper and concentrated on the issue of reporting restrictions. This case is reported separately.

vi) Following a proposal by magistrates themselves, analysis of comments made in 'log books' kept in the Youth Court.

Rotherham, Leicester City court, Market Bosworth court and Ashby de la Zouch provided 'log books' at the Youth Courts for the duration of the project, in which magistrates and other court users could record their comments and suggestions about the new arrangements. The comments recorded in the first few months of 1999 were analysed for their content. (The periods covered in this analysis are: Rotherham, 4 February to 7 April 1999; Leicester City court 3 March to 28 April 1999; Ashby de la Zouch 7 January to 6 May 1999; Market Bosworth court 20 January to 29 April 1999.) Except at Market Bosworth court, the majority of comments came from magistrates.

vii) A telephone survey of courts elsewhere in the country where related developments had occurred or been considered

In addition to Rotherham and Leicestershire, eight other court areas indicated an interest in the Demonstration Project to the Home Office and Lord Chancellor's Department, and two others expressed an interest in the project to the researchers. They were advised that, although they had not been chosen to pilot the project, they could still try out aspects of it. These courts were therefore contacted by the researchers to ascertain whether any of their experiences were relevant to the Demonstration Project.

Appendix B   Details of court observations

Characteristics of the sample

Altogether 1,293 hearings were observed in the two court areas between October 1998 to September 1999 (the initial study period) and February and March 2000 (the follow-up period). The distribution of these hearings was as shown in Table B.1.

Of these hearings the majority, just over 70 per cent, were cases in progress, with just under 30 per cent being hearings where offenders were sentenced. This distinction is an important one in the context of the present study since, other things being equal, magistrates would be expected to engage more with offenders at the point where they are determining sentence. Therefore, in analysing the court observations data most attention has been paid to hearings where sentence was determined.

In eight out of every ten hearings the bench was entirely composed of lay magistrates, with a stipendiary sitting in 12 per cent of the hearings, and a mixed bench in 7 per cent of the hearings. In this analysis no distinction has been made between the different compositions of the bench.

As Tables B.2 to B.4 show, the majority of defendants observed at hearings were aged 16 or 17 (more than 60%), male (86% overall) and white (88%)

Examining engagement

One of the main purposes of the observations was to examine the extent to which engagement changed as result of the Demonstration Project. In order to examine this important distinctions have been made. As explained above, for legal reasons magistrates are inhibited to some extent in what they can say prior to a finding of guilt, therefore most interest focuses on what engagement occurred in hearings where sentencing took place. Also, it was known from the start of the study that the number of hearings that it would be possible to observe in individual Youth Courts in the county of Leicestershire during the period of the Demonstration Project would be too few to make it possible to analyse changes occurring at each and every court. Therefore the courts in the county in Leicestershire have been grouped together, and most of the tables that follow analyse the data for Rotherham, Leicestershire city and Leicestershire county. In most of the analyses statistical significance has been tested by comparing means using an analysis of variance with a Bonferroni test, a modified least significant difference test.

Table B.1: Number of cases observed at each court

Month	Rotherham	Leicester City	Market Bosworth	Ashby de la Zouch	Lough-borough	Melton Mowbray	Total
Oct 98	40	7	6	-	-	-	53
Nov 98	35	38	-	5	2	-	80
Dec 98	17	44	-	-	-	-	61
Jan 99	18	18	5	-	2	-	43
Feb 99	77	38	8	4	-	-	127
Mar 99	51	63	-	-	6	-	120
Apr 99	47	43	-	-	9	-	99
May 99	52	33	5	-	4	-	94
Jun 99	61	38	5	6	-	-	110
Jul 99	66	29	-	-	4	8	107
Aug 99	41	53	4	-	-	-	98
Sep 99	69	16	-	-	-	-	85
Feb – Mar 00	96	88	12	7	9	4	216
Total number	670	508	45	22	36	12	1,293
percentage	52	39	3	2	3	1	100

Table B.2: Percentage of defendants of each age observed at each court

Age	Rotherham	Leicester City	Market Bosworth	Ashby de la Zouch	Lough-borough	Melton Mowbray	All Courts
10	1	-	-	-	-	-	<1
11	2	-	-	-	-	-	1
12	1	2	2	-	3	-	1
13	4	7	7	9	-	17	5
14	9	10	9	9	6	33	9
15	18	18	21	18	20	-	18
16	33	29	14	36	31	17	31
17	29	32	37	27	34	33	31
18	3	2	9	-	3	-	3
19	-	-	-	-	3	-	<1
Number	669	479	43	22	35	12	1,260
Average age	16	16	16	16	16	15	16

Note: The age of defendants is not known in 33 instances.

Table B.3: *Percentage of female defendants observed at each court*

	Rotherham	Leicester City	Market Bosworth	Ashby de la Zouch	Lough-borough	Melton Mowbray	All Courts
female	17	12	4	18	11	-	14

Table B.4: *Race of defendants observed at each court*

Ethnic Group	Rotherham	Leicester City	Market Bosworth	Ashby de la Zouch	Lough-borough	Melton Mowbray	Total
White	96	75	96	100	97	100	88
Black	<1	10	4	-	-	-	4
Asian	1	8	-	-	3	-	4
Mixed	<1	6	-	-	-	-	3
Unknown	2	<1	-	-	-	-	1

Did Magistrates Talk to Defendants More ?

Table B.5: Mean number of times that magistrates talked to defendants, by court areas and month, for sentencing hearings

Month	Rotherham	Leicestershire City	Leicestershire County
Oct 98	14	16	6
Nov 98	16	9	19
Dec 98	19	6	-
Jan 99	14	9	10
Feb 99	15	9	23
Mar 99	21	9	22
Apr 99	17	12	13
May 99	19	14	9
Jun 99	20	8	14
Jul 99	17	9	12
Aug 99	16	11	13
Sep 99	14	6	-
Feb - Mar 00	23	15	12
Total number	342	119	34

Note:
In Rotherham the follow-up period was significantly different to February and September 1999 (F = 3.67, p < .0001).
In Leicestershire there were no statistically significant differences in either city or county Youth Courts.

Table B.5 suggests fluctuations in the number of times that magistrates talked to defendants rather than a clear pattern of increasing engagement. It is, however, worth noting that in Rotherham the number of times that magistrates talked to defendants was higher during the follow-up period than at any other time, and markedly higher than at the beginning of the project. One possible explanation is that it took a long time for the project to have a discernible impact. However, it is also possible that the follow-up period was no more than another upward fluctuation, rather than an established pattern.

Did magistrates ask defendants questions more?

Talking to defendants in general may not carry any great importance. But did magistrates seek to engage defendants more by asking more questions following the start of the project?

Table B.6: *Mean number of times that magistrates asked defendants questions, by court areas and month, for sentencing hearings*

Month	Rotherham	Leicestershire City	Leicestershire County
Oct 98	1	9	2
Nov 98	3	2	10
Dec 98	2	2	-
Jan 99	3	3	4
Feb 99	3	3	14
Mar 99	6	3	13
Apr 99	4	4	8
May 99	6	8	3
Jun 99	8	4	8
Jul 99	4	4	6
Aug 99	8	6	9
Sep 99	3	2	-
Feb – Mar 00	9	10	6
Total number	346	120	34

Note:
In Rotherham the follow-up period was significantly different to October and November 1998, and January, February, April, July and September 1999. ($F = 6.23$, $p < .001$).
In Leicestershire city the follow-up period was significantly different to December 1998 ($F = 2.30$, $p < .01$), and in Leicestershire county there were no statistically significant differences.

As before, there is no consistent upward trend, although again during the follow-up period Rotherham had a higher mean number of questions asked than at the beginning of the project. Leicester city Youth Court had small peaks, and Leicestershire county Youth Courts had a more noticeable peak during the spring of 1999, which coincided with sessions to give magistrates some training in engaging with young offenders.

It is possible that it was not the average amount of questioning that changed, but the fact that magistrates would be likely to ask questions at all. Table B.7 shows the proportion of occasions in a particular month when magistrates asked offenders no questions.

Table B.7: ***Proportion of times that magistrates asked defendants no questions, by court areas and month, for sentencing hearings***

Month	Rotherham	Leicestershire City	Leicestershire County
Oct 98	57	50	0
Nov 98	21	70	0
Dec 98	0	71	0
Jan 99	14	25	0
Feb 99	12	14	0
Mar 99	6	19	0
Apr 99	17	33	0
May 99	0	33	33
Jun 99	0	40	0
Jul 99	6	25	0
Aug 99	0	33	0
Sep 99	10	33	0
Feb – Mar 00	6	13	0
Total number	192	120	34

Here there does appear to be a trend emerging, although various interpretations are possible. In Rotherham there appears to be an immediate impact of the Demonstration Project. However, because it was not possible to obtain a baseline of what happened prior to the start of the project it is not known to what extent October 1998 was typical of pre-Project practice. In Leicester there was a similar decline. In the Youth Courts in the county in Leicestershire, by contrast, it appears that throughout the study period magistrates asked at least one question when sentencing young offenders. This may be because there was already an established practice of questioning young offenders prior to the project. One further qualification to be noted is that Table B.7 sometimes involved quite small numbers.

Did Magistrates Talk to Defendants' Families More ?

Table B.8: ***Mean number of times that magistrates asked defendants' family questions, by court areas and month, for sentencing hearings***

Month	Rotherham	Leicestershire City	Leicestershire County
Oct 98	1	2	2
Nov 98	1	0	2
Dec 98	4	< 1	-
Jan 99	2	2	1
Feb 99	2	2	4
Mar 99	1	3	0
Apr 99	1	5	0
May 99	2	3	2
Jun 99	2	2	2
Jul 99	3	3	5
Aug 99	4	1	2
Sep 99	2	< 1	-
Feb – Mar 00	4	1	3
Total number	139	83	23

Note:

In the city court in Leicestershire magistrates asked significantly more questions of defendants families in April 1999 than in November and December 1998 ($F = 2.56$, $p < .007$). Otherwise there was no change.

Did Defendants Talk More?

One of the aspects of the project that attracted most support was the idea that the young offender should no longer be a passive observer of proceedings. Therefore did offenders talk more in court?

Table B.9: *Mean number of times that defendants talked, by court areas and month, for sentencing hearings*

Month	Rotherham	Leicestershire City	Leicestershire County
Oct 98	16	15	7
Nov 98	14	12	19
Dec 98	20	8	-
Jan 99	16	11	11
Feb 99	15	11	23
Mar 99	20	12	25
Apr 99	17	14	30
May 99	20	16	13
Jun 99	21	11	18
Jul 99	16	14	16
Aug 99	18	12	17
Sep 99	13	10	-
Feb – Mar 00	25	20	15
Total number	342	119	34

Note:

In Rotherham the follow-up period was significantly different to November 1998 and February, July and September 1999 (F = 3.80, p < .001).

In Leicestershire city and Leicestershire county analysis of variance was not statistically significant.

In Rotherham and Leicester city court the amount that young offenders talked in the course of sentencing hearings was higher during the follow-up period than at any time since the start of the project. In the courts in the county of Leicestershire the amount of talking by young offenders during the follow-up period was twice what it had been at the start of the project, but not as great as it had been during February to April 1999, suggesting that, as with the number of questions that magistrates asked offenders (Table B.6), offender involvement peaked around the time that training courses were taking place.

Duration of hearings

At the beginning of the project some concern was expressed that if magistrates did engage more with defendants then this might result in longer hearings, at a time when courts were being urged to deal with cases as swiftly as possible and reduce delay in the system.

Table B.10: Mean number of minutes that hearings lasted, by court areas and month, for sentencing and other hearings

Month	Rotherham		Leicestershire City		Leicestershire County	
	Sentence	Other	Sentence	Other	Sentence	Other
Nov 98	33	8	18	9	21	17
Dec 98	28	10	30	12	-	-
Jan 99	15	8	28	9	32	21
Feb 99	21	20	22	9	38	21
Mar 99	44	7	26	7	16	13
Apr 99	22	10	20	15	10	11
May 99	18	9	35	13	30	20
Jun 99	20	11	45	13	27	30
Jul 99	43	8	26	11	39	26
Aug 99	10	6	25	12	24	3
Sep 99	16	8	14	5	-	-
Feb-Mar 00	28	10	34	11	25	13
Total number	175	402	110	311	30	58

Note:
In Rotherham for sentenced hearings there were significant differences between March 1999 and February, May and June 1999, and between July and September 1999 ($F = 3.59$, $p < .001$). However, this appears to indicate large fluctuations in the times of hearings, rather than a consistent pattern of increased length of hearings resulting from the Demonstration Project. There were no differences in the other area.i

Comments

To summarise, in hearings where young offenders were sentenced, there was no clearly identifiable and consistent pattern suggesting that, in general, magistrates talked to young offenders more following the start of the project, or asked them or their families more questions on average. However, there were indications that some changes did take place. Although the average *amount* of questions did not increase in a consistent manner, the occasions on which magistrates asked *no* questions decreased, suggesting that it was not so much that there was an overall increase in questioning, as that magistrates did at least ask some questions where previously they might have asked none.

There was also some evidence that (apart from the Youth Courts in the county in Leicestershire) young offenders participated by talking more than hitherto. It was also noticeable that there were more changes in interaction in Rotherham than in Leicestershire, and that where changes did occur they were most in evidence during the follow-up period, suggesting that it may have taken some time for any shift in approach to work its way through. It was found that despite the project's objective of encouraging greater engagement, there did not appear to be any general increase in the length of time that hearings lasted. This is encouraging if courts are also expected to deal with cases as speedily as possible, and it is consistent with the indications that the overall amount of questioning did not increase, but rather that magistrates may have asked one or two questions where previously they asked none.

These comments need to be viewed with caution since, despite the large number of hearings observed, the findings should be regarded as indicative rather than conclusive. This is because it is hard to know whether the changes that were observed could be attributed directly to the impact of the Demonstration Project. Despite differences being statistically significant, it is possible that they reflected fluctuations and variability in practice rather than a cause and effect consequence of the project. In particular, there were no baseline data so that comparisons could not be made with a similar period preceding the initiation of the project.

Appendix C   Details of the case studies

	Rotherham		Leicestershire	
	number	percentage	number	percentage
Case studies	20	100	20	100
Age				
12	1	5	1	5
13	1	5	0	0
14	3	15	2	10
15	6	30	3	15
16	2	10	4	20
17	7	35	10	50
Gender				
Male	16	80	18	90
Female	4	20	2	10
Race				
Afro-Caribbean	0	0	0	0
Asian	0	0	1	5
Mixed	0	0	2	10
White	20	100	17	85
Convictions				
No Previous	5	25	7	35
Previous	15	75	13	65
Most Serious Offence				
Violence	1	5	2	10
Sexual Offence	0	0	1	5
Burglary	2	10	1	5
Theft	8	40	8	40
Vehicle Offence	5	25	4	20
Possession of Drugs	0	0	1	5
Public Order	0	0	2	10
Intimidate Witness	1	5	0	0
Nuisance	0	0	1	5
Criminal Damage	3	15	0	0
Sentence*				
Custody	0	0	1	5
Probation	2	10	2	10
Combination Order	0	0	1	5
Supervision Order	3	15	2	10
Attendance Centre	3	15	4	20
Disqualified (driving)	1	5	2	10
Licence Endorsed	3	15	1	5
Compensation Order	2	10	2	10
Fine	5	25	3	15
Court Costs	3	15	7	35
Conditional Discharge	5	25	6	30
Deferred	1	5	1	5

Note: Some offenders received more than one sentence.

	Rotherham		Leicestershire	
	number	percentage	number	percentage
Support *				
Mother	10	50	7	35
Father	0	0	7	35
Step-father	1	5	0	0
Foster-father	1	5	0	0
Grandmother	1	5	0	0
Grandfather	2	10	0	0
Aunt	0	0	1	5
Cousin	1	5	0	0
Brother	0	0	1	5
Attendance Centre Officer	0	0	1	5
None	5	25	7	35

Note: * Some offenders were accompanied to court by more than one supporter.

Rotherham Youth Court panel protocol

(i) Engaging young offenders and their parents more effectively

Appropriate stage for intervention?

ONLY after plea of guilty or finding of guilt after a trial – not appropriate to address issues re: <u>alleged</u> behaviour pre-conviction.

However, <u>Chairmen</u> should speak with young person charged and parent(s)/guardians at OUTSET once brought by Usher – <u>briefly</u> introduce people in court and their roles/how hearing will be conducted (no need to make specific reference to a victim/press at outset). Stress importance and seriousness of occasion and that young person and parents are the focus of the courtroom. Inform young person and parent(s) when to sit/stand in court and when they will be invited to speak or ask questions. Stress that the young offender is here because of what he has done, not because of who he is.

The invite the Court Clerk to explain the substance of the charge – simple language – consistent with age, maturity, understanding of young person.

- At this early stage Chairman to stress important role of defence solicitor (where appropriate)

- Following conviction the Chairman should attempt wherever deemed appropriate, to engage with the young offender and his/her parent(s) focusing on the former's offending behaviour and how to change it.

Where communication takes place between the Chairman and the young offender and/or his parent(s) the defence solicitor should be invited to have the 'last word'.

Chairmen and colleagues will need to recognise that some young offenders will either be physically/mentally unable to engage in conversation or may simply decline to do so – inferences adverse to young offenders should not be drawn from their failure to engage in this way.

Family Proceedings court style court layout may be considered appropriate by the Panel, in cases other than young offenders who are IN CUSTODY – in these cases the security risks inherent in the less formal case setting are usually likely to exceed any benefit which might otherwise be gained. It may be appropriate to begin the project with magistrates remaining on the Bench and at some point early in the New Year experimenting with a 'family proceedings' style layout in appropriate cases.

There should be a presumption that a young offender in custody will be outside the scope of the less formal layout – if the Bench are considering otherwise in an individual case it would be appropriate to invite representations from the CPS (through whom Group 4 may pass on their concerns), defence solicitors and court clerks.

There is no reason why Chairmen should not attempt to engage in ALL young offenders irrespective of the courtroom layout and whether they are in custody, care or on bail.

Youth Justice social workers, defence solicitors and court clerks have agreed to liaise even more closely than at present in order to assist the Crown in determining whether it would be appropriate to attempt to engage the young offender and his parent(s) in each individual case, post conviction and as to how best the communication can be managed in order to have the highest likelihood of being effective.

ALWAYS REMEMBER THAT MAGISTRATES ARE MEMBERS OF THE JUDICIARY AND ARE SITTING IN A YOUTH <u>COURT</u>, NOT A COMMITTEE.

(ii) (a) Allowing victims to attend Youth Court proceedings

It seems clear that Section 47 of the C.Y.P.A. 1933 permits the Bench to admit victims to sit in Court to observe cases in which they are directly concerned – their "direct concern" stems from the 'status' as a 'victim of crime'.

Similarly, a parent or friend accompanying a victim and/or a Witness Support volunteer can also be permitted to attend with the victim.

The Bench will need to judge on the merits of each case whether the victim(s) of a particular case should be allowed to attend a Youth Court trial if they so wish, and should decline such a request ONLY if the particular circumstances of the case lead you to conclude that it would be contrary to the wider interests of justice so to allow.

In reaching their conclusions the Bench should as a matter of good practice, always invite representatives from the CPS, defence, Youth Justice representatives and court clerk.

Some or all of the following factors may assist Benches in concluding that victims should not be permitted to attend all or part of the proceedings in the Youth Court:

● age, maturity, vulnerability of the defendant

● the number of victims involved in the case

● the sensitivity or personal nature of information about the offender which may be discussed at the sentencing stage – e.g. sensitive issues contained in a P.S.R.

There may, therefore, be some occasions when a victim observes a trial, hears the bench announce conviction and then is asked to leave court for several minutes while particularly sensitive issues are considered. The victim should then be invited back into court for the pronouncement of sentence.

Magistrates will again wish to hear representations from the person referred to above before reaching decisions in this sensitive area.

The question is one of BALANCE between the benefits of openness and the promotion of public confidence in the Youth Justice system as against the rights of the individual defendant/young offender.

(ii) (b)   Allowing the public to attend Youth Court proceedings

Youth courts are not "open courts" in the same way as adult magistrates' courts are. However, the Government believes that the public should be allowed to attend Youth Court proceedings in certain circumstances – e.g.:

● Where a young person's offending has impacted on a number of people in a locality or the local community in general – e.g. persistent burglar, taker of vehicles without consent, dealing drugs etc.

Requests from members of the public to attend Youth Courts are likely to be rare, however, each such request should be carefully considered on its merits.

Again the bench should invite representation from the above mentioned persons before reaching a decision on whether or not to admit member(s) of the public.

Again there is a balance to be reached here between the court holding real dialogue with an offender (post-conviction) and the aim to open up the Youth Courts to promote public confidence in the system.

The factors set out above in relation to allowing victims to attend and observe Youth Courts are equally applicable here.

(iii) The Press and the lifting of reporting restrictions in the Youth Court (post conviction)

The Press have a statutory right to be present at all Youth Court hearings and have freedom to report the proceedings subject to proviso that they must not identify the children or young persons involved.

Youth Courts now possess the STATUTORY power to dispense with the restriction on publication of reports of proceedings in the press (T.V. etc) where:

a. The child/young person has been CONVICTED; and

b. It is in the public interest to do so.

The court must hear representations CPS, defence and court clerks <u>before</u> making such an order.

Considerations:

- Need to prevent further offending by the young person – consistent with the need to have regard to the welfare of the young person;

- Lifting of reporting restrictions might be particularly appropriate where:

- The nature of the young person's offending is persistent or serious or has impacted on a number of people in his/her community in general.

- Altering others to the young person's behaviour would help to prevent further offending by him/her.

- Lifting of restrictions might be particularly inappropriate when:

  ❑ Naming the young offender would reveal identity of a vulnerable victim and lead to unwelcome publicity for that victim.

  ❑ Publicity may put the offender or his/her family at risk of harassment or harm.

  ❑ Offender is particularly young or vulnerable

  ❑ Offender is contrite and has shown him/herself to accept responsibility for his/her actions – e.g. by a timely plea of guilty (where such a plea is appropriate).

Letter sent to all panel members in Rotherham

<u>Demonstration Project "Changing the Culture of the Youth Court"</u>

Effectively engaging with young offenders (and parents) with the purpose of encouraging offenders to take responsibility for their offending.

The following points were raised by members of the panel and representatives of other agencies present at the panel meeting on the 9th November which all members of the Youth Panel and in particular the Chairman may find of particular value:

- Introductory questions regarding the offender's family/school/behaviour which may assist to begin the engaging process, i.e. there is not need to go straight to the "heart of the matter" PROVIDED THAT THE ENGAGING DOES NOT JUST STOP THERE;

- Questions can helpfully be addressed towards the young offender's attitude to his/her victims/concequences of his/her offending behaviour ec., "e.g. What would you think/how would you feel if the person you assaulted/stole from/burgled etc. was your grandmother...?";

- It was noted that there is need to take care not to reach sentencing conclusions based solely on the parent's view;

- Particularly in cases where the offender is the eldest in the family, questions such as, "What example are you setting your younger brothers/sisters?" and "What effect do you think you offending and coming before the court is having on your mother/father?" may be of positive value in the engaging process;

- Try to keep all questions "open" so far as possible, i.e. try not to ask questions which illicit "yes/no" replies.

Other questions which might assist in the engaging process were suggested as follows:

- What do you think/feel might stop you offending in the future?

- If you were sitting where I am dealing with you, how would you deal with your case?

- What can you do to make sure you do not offend in the future?

Finally, it was re-emphasised that there is a need to try, so far as possible, to use simple language that young offenders and parents can understand and avoid using jargon.

The above is by no means an exhaustive list but, hopefully, pulls together some of the types of questions and approaches which you and your colleagues have found to be particularly successful in at least some of the cases you have dealt with over the last 12 months or so.

Leicester City Youth Court Panel Protocol

This Protocol has been adopted by the combined Youth Court Panel as part of the pilot project aiming to change the culture of the youth courts. Amongst the objectives of the youth court are:

- By making the court less formal, and otherwise engaging offenders to ensure they face up to the consequences of their offending behaviour;

- Engaging parents of young offenders;

- Ensuring the public, and victims of crime, are better informed as to the work of the court, and lifting reporting restrictions enabling offenders to be identified where it is appropriate and in the public interest; and

- Developing mechanisms for the feedback of information to sentencers.

This protocol will take effect from the 1st March 1999 until further notice.

COURT LAYOUT

1.1. The arrangement of furniture in the court may be changed from time to time to encourage offenders and their parents to participate in proceedings.

1.2. Changes to the layout will be made after consultation with the Bench and users.

1.3. Changes will not be made where they would reduce the security of magistrates or court users.

2.   DEFENDANTS

2.1. Defendants will only be required to stand in court when the charges are put to them and when sentencing is passed. During the rest of the proceedings they should be allowed to remain seated.

2.2. The chairman should make it clear to defendants who have been *convicted* that he or she may be asking them questions during the course of the proceedings. The purpose of questioning is to:

a) ensure the bench has all the relevant information before sentencing; and

b) to encourage the offender to recognise his or her wrongdoing.

The chairman should not deliver homilies when sentencing.

PARENTS AND GUARDIANS

2.3. Parents and guardians may be seated throughout the proceedings involving a youth for whom they care save they should be invited to stand when the chairman is announcing orders which affect them personally (e.g. binding them over to take care and control of their children, making them responsible for financial penalties and ensuring they complete Court Orders).

2.4. Parents and guardians should be encouraged to address the court directly *when the defendant has been convicted.*

WITNESSES

2.5. Witnesses should be asked to stand whilst taking the Oath and thereafter be invited to sit whilst they give their evidence.

2.6. Where parties are aware that a witness is worried about appearing in court, contact should be made with the Witness Service so that appropriate arrangements can be made.

3. Victims

3.1. The alleged victims of a crime will usually be entitled to attend Youth Court proceedings as people directly concerned with the proceedings.

4. Attendance of Others

6.1. The court may give permission for people not directly concerned with the case or otherwise entitled to be present in the court, where it feels this is appropriate. Where a person wishes to be allowed into the Youth Court, he or she should notify the Court Usher. The Court Usher will tell the Legal Advisor and the person will be asked to come into court when the case in which they are interested is called on. The Chairman will invite the person wishing to remain to outline their reasons to determine the application.

6.2. When determining such an application, the Court will take account of the reasons put forward by the applicant and the likely effects on the proceedings. Prosecutors and defence advocates will be entitled to make representation as to the propriety of the Court allowing the applicant to remain.

EXCLUSION FROM THE COURT

4.1. Those who have been permitted to observe proceedings should not be routinely excluded during the course of the proceedings. The Court may, however, order the court to be cleared where Section 37 of the Children and Young Persons Act 1933 applies, in any case concerning proceedings in relation to an offence against, or any conduct contrary to, decency or morality, where a child or young person is called as a witness.

ADVOCATES

4.2. Advocates and other court officers (e.g. Social Workers and Probation Officers) will be invited to remain seated throughout the proceedings.

4.3. The Chairman should make it clear to Advocates that they may be asking questions directly of their clients *once convicted*.

MEDIA

4.4. Members of the Press are entitled to be present in the Youth Court and their attendance in Court is encouraged.

4.5. The Court Office will provide lists of cases to be heard in the Youth Court to the local Press whose responsibility it will be to ensure that the prohibition on the identification of youths is observed.

4.6. Supplemented lists will be made available to members of the Press on the day of the hearing.

4.7. Court Ushers and Legal Advisors will endeavour to make members of the Press aware when cases are transferred from one court to another, particularly where those reporters have expressed and interest in a particular case.

4.8. The Court may lift reporting restrictions *where offenders have been convicted* and it is in the public interest to do so, the Court may then make such an order on application or of its own motion.

4.8.1. If the court is considering lifting reporting restrictions it should invite the parties and members of the press present to make representations.

4.8.2. The police may make application to the Court to lift reporting restrictions through the Crown Prosecutor.

4.8.3. The Prosecutor may make the application on his or her own behalf.

4.8.4. The Press may make application to lift reporting restrictions. If a number of reporters are present, they should chose one of their number on speak on their behalf when making applications or representations to the Court.

4.8.5. Where the Press wish to be heard or make application they should notify the Legal Advisor prior to the case being called on.

Loughborough and Melton Mowbray combined Youth Court Panel Protocol

This protocol has been adopted by the Combined Youth Court Panel at its meeting on Tuesday 30th March 1999 as part of the project aiming at changing the culture in the Youth Courts. The objectives are to:

- *Make the Youth Court less formal ensuring that defendants face up to the consequences of their offending behaviour;*

- *Create an atmosphere which encourages dialogue between defendants, parents and guardians and the Court;*

- *Increases awareness on the part of victims of crime and the public of the work of the Youth Court;*

- *Encourage Youth Courts to consider the desirability of otherwise of lifting reporting restrictions within the provisions of Section 49 of the Children and Youth Persons Act 1933;*

- *Develop mechanisms for the feedback of information to sentencers.*

COURT LAYOUT

1.1. Diagrams were attached to the protocol illustrating the changed layouts of the courts.

2. Defendants

2.1. Defendants will be required to stand in Court only when the charges are put and when sentence is passed. During the rest of the proceedings they should normally be allowed to remain seated.

2.2. The Chairman will make it clear to defendants who have been found guilty that they may be asked questions by the bench during the course of the proceedings to:

a) ensure the Bench has all the relevant information before sentencing; and

b) to encourage the offender to recognise his or her wrongdoing.

3.   Parents and Guardians

3.1. Parents and guardians may be seated throughout the proceedings. However, they should be invited to stand when the Chairman announces a decision which affect parents and guardians (for example parental bindovers and payment of financial penalties).

3.2. Parents and guardians will be encouraged to address the court directly.

4.   WITNESSES

4.1. Witnesses will be asked to stand when taking the Oath but invited to sit to give evidence.

5.   VICTIMS

5.1. Victims of crime will usually be entitled to attend Youth Court Proceedings as either witnesses or persons directly concerned with the proceedings.

6.   ATTENDANCE OF OTHERS

6.1. The court may give permission for people not directly concerned with the case or otherwise entitled to be present in the Court, where appropriate. Where such a person wishes to come into the Youth Court, he or she should notify the Court Usher. The Court Usher will inform the Legal Adviser who will give directions as appropriate. The chairman will invite the person wishing to remain to outline to the bench their reasons for wishing to attend.

7.   ADVOCATES

7.1. Advocates and other court officers (e.g. Social Workers and Probation Officers) will be asked to remain seated throughout the proceedings.

7.2. Unless the court considers it inappropriate the Chairman will question defendants after finding of guilt whether legally represented or not.

8.   MEDIA

8.1. Members of the press are entitled to be present in the Youth Court and their attendance in Court is encouraged.

8.2. The Court Office will make available to the local press lists of cases to be heard in the Youth Court.

8.3. Supplementary lists will be available to members of the Press on the day of the hearing.

8.4. The Court Legal Advisors and Court Ushers will ensure that interested parties are made aware when cases are transferred from one Court to another.

8.5. In accordance with the provisions of Section 49 of the Children and Youth Persons Act 1933the court may lift reporting restrictions where offenders have been found guilty and it is in the public interest to do so, after considering the following:

- The nature of the young person's offending is persistent or serious or has impacted on a number of people or his or her local community in general;

- Altering others to the young person's behaviour would help prevent further offending by him or her;

- Naming the young offender would reveal the identity of a vulnerable victim and lead to unwelcome publicity for that victim;

- Publicity may put the offender or his/her family at risk of harassment or harm;

- The offender is particularly young or vulnerable;

- The offender is contrite and has shown him or herself ready to accept responsibility for his or her actions by, for example, an early guilty plea.

8.6 If the court is considering lifting reporting restrictions it will usually invite the parties and members of the Press present to make oral representations.

8.7 Where the Press wish to be heard or make an application to the court the Legal Adviser should be notified before the case is called on.

Market Bosworth and Ashby de la Zouch Combined Youth Court Panel Protocol

This protocol has been adapted by the Combined Youth Court Panel at a meeting held on the 21st October, 1999 as part of a project aiming at changing the culture in the Youth Courts. The objectives are to:

- *Make the Youth Court less formal and otherwise engaging offenders to ensure they face up to the consequences of their offending behaviour;*

- *Engage the parents of young offenders;*

- *Ensure the public and victims of crime are better informed as to the work of the Court and lifting reporting restrictions enabling offenders to be identified where it is appropriate and in the public interests; and*

- *Develop mechanisms for the feedback of information to sentencers.*

COURT LAYOUT

1.1. As agreed.

2.   DEFENDANTS

2.1. Defendants will be required to stand in Court only when the charges are put and when sentence is passed. During the rest of the proceedings they should normally be allowed to remain seated.

2.2. The Chairman should make it clear to defendants who have been found guilty that they may be asked questions by the Bench during the course of the proceedings to:

c) ensure the Bench has all the relevant information before sentencing; and

d) to encourage the offender to recognise his or her wrongdoing.

3.   Parents and Guardians

3.1. Parents and guardians may be seated throughout the proceedings involving a youth for whom they care. However, they should be invited to stand when the Chairman announces orders which affect parents and guardians (for example parental bindovers and payment of financial penalties).

3.2. Parents and guardians should be encouraged to address the court directly.

4.   WITNESSES

4.1. Witnesses will be asked to stand when taking the Oath but invited to sit to give evidence.

5.   VICTIMS

5.1. Alleged victims of a crime will usually be entitled to attend Youth Court Proceedings as either witnesses or persons directly concerned with the proceedings.

6.   ATTENDANCE OF OTHERS

6.1. The court may give permission for people not directly concerned with the case or otherwise entitled to be present in the Court where appropriate. Where such a person wishes to be allowed into the Youth Court, he or she should notify the Court Usher. The Court Usher will liaise with the Legal Adviser with a view to bringing the interested party before the Court. The chairman will invite the person wishing to remain to address the Bench.

7.   ADVOCATES

7.1. Advocates and other Court Officers (e.g. Social Workers and Probation Officers) will be invited to remain seated throughout the proceedings.

7.2. The Chairman should make it clear to Advocates the the Bench may ask questions directly of their client after finding of guilt.

8.   MEDIA

8.1. Members of the press are entitled to be present in the Youth Court and their attendance in Court is encouraged.

8.2. The Court Office will provide lists of cases to be heard in the Youth Court to the local Press, whose responsibility it will be to ensure that the prohibition on the identification of youths is observed.

8.3. Supplementary lists will be available to members of the Press on the day of the hearing.

8.4. Legal Advisors and Court Ushers will endeavour to make members of the Press aware when cases are transferred from one Court to another, particularly where those reporters have expressed an interest in a particular case.

8.5. The Court may lift reporting restrictions where offenders have been found guilty and it is on the public interest to do so.

8.6. If the court is considering lifting reporting restrictions, it will normally invite the parties and members of the Press present to make representations.

8.7. Where the Press wishes to be heard or make an application, it should notify the Legal Advisor prior to the case being called on.

Appendix E

An example newsletter

SENTENCING IN LEICESTERSHIRE AND RUTLAND IN 1997

Twelve per cent of 14-17 year olds who appeared before the youth court in 1997 received some form of custodial sentence. In total 57 % of 14-17 year olds received some form of community sentence, 11 % were fined and 13 % received a discharge.

The most common sentence for 10-13 year olds was an attendance centre order (table 1).

Table 1: Sentencing of 10-13 year olds. 1997

Leicestershire and Rutland MCC

Order	Indictable	All offences	
	No.	No.	%
Supervision	3	13	24
Attendance Centre	2	20	36
Fine	0	3	5
Discharge	6	18	33
All	11	55	100

How does this compare with sentencing elsewhere?

Leicestershire and Rutland imposed custody for a slightly higher proportion of young offenders than the national figure of 8 % (Fig. 1). The courts made more use of community sentences than the national average but close inspection shows that this was due to the high number of attendance centre orders made.

Leicestershire and Rutland imposed attendance centre orders in 26% of cases where the offender was sentenced for an indictable offence compared to 11% of cases nationally.

Discharges were used in a much smaller proportion of indictable offences than nationally.

One possible explanation for this is that the diversion scheme means that cases that would receive a discharge for in other areas are diverted away from court. Alternatively it may be that cases that may have been dealt with by a discharge are receiving attendance centre orders instead.

Committals to the Crown Court for sentence

The court commits young offenders to the Crown Court at six times the national rate: 10% of those charged with indictable offences are committed for sentence to the higher court compared to 1.5% elsewhere.

THE EFFECTIVENESS OF SENTENCING: NATIONAL FIGURES

Cautioning

Among those cautioned, only 22% of young men and 11% of young women are convicted of a further offence within 2 years. This proportion has remained about the same since 1985.

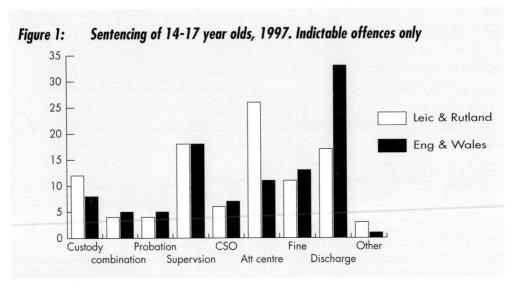

Figure 1: *Sentencing of 14-17 year olds, 1997. Indictable offences only*

MEASURING SUCCESS

Where there are such high rates of reconviction, you need to be realistic about how you will measure 'success'. In many cases, it is unrealistic to expect that young offender will not reconvicted of any offence. But we can take signs that they are 'growing out of crime' as indicators that any intervention is being successful:

- Are recent offences less serious than earlier offending?
- Is he or she offending at a slower rate than previously?
- Are there any signs that he or she is settling down (e.g. attending school more often, started a job or training.

Remember that it is unrealistic to expect them to stop offending straight away. It will take time for any intervention to be effective.

COMPLETION OF COMMUNITY SENTENCES

We do not know what proportion of community sentences are completed nationally. However, the local youth justice agencies have provided some figures for 1998. ('Completed' means that the order was not breached).

83% of the 109 orders supervised by Leicestershire and Rutland Probation Service were either completed successfully or are in the process of being completed.

Leicestershire and Rutland junior attendance centre received 161 orders in 1998. 76% were completed.

Figures for Jan – June 1998 found that 71% of supervision orders supervised by Leicestershire County Youth Justice Team were either completed or in the process of being completed. 69% of these offenders were not reconvicted within 6 months.

Leicester City SSD studied a sample of 25 supervision orders starting in Jan-June 1998. They found that 72% had not been reconvicted after three months. In March 1999, half of these orders had been completed successfully. Most of the others are still on going.

NATIONAL STANDARDS FOR COMMUNITY SENTENCES

The national standards for community sentences state that there should be 5 days between the order being imposed and the first meeting. A written sentence plan should be agreed with the offender within 10 days of the order being imposed.

Table 2 shows the time to starting a community sentence for orders imposed at the youh court in 1998.

Leicestershire Junior Attendance Centre
The average time between imposition of an order and first appointment is 3 weeks. It can accept an order with 5 days notice.

Table 2: Average time to starting a community sentence

	No. Orders Starting in 1998	% offenders seen within 5 working days of order commencing	% sentence plans within 10 working days of order commencing
Leic. & Rutland Probation[1] (16-17 year olds)	52	58	50
Leicestershire County SSD[2] (10-15 year olds)	28	88	80
Leicester City SSD[3]	25	84	80

1. No information available on CSOs. Data for the last quarter of 1998. Excludes cases where information is unavailable.
2. Figures for Jan-June 1998.
3. Sample of 25 supervision orders beginning in Jan-June 1998.

Court sentences

The lowest reconviction rates are for fines and discharges (Fig. 2). Just under three-quarters of offenders aged 14-17 sentenced to community service and attendance centres were reconvicted within two years. 79% of young offenders given supervision orders and 87% of under-18s given probation were reconvicted within the next two years. 81% of offenders receiving a custodial sentence were reconvicted in the two years following their release.

However, research has found that, when the age and previous record of offenders are accounted for, there is very little difference in reconviction rates between sentences.

Age and patterns of reconviction

There is a general pattern of reconviction rates declining with age. For example, 58% of 18-20-year-olds sentenced to a CSO in 1994 were reconvicted within two years compared to 74% of under-18s. Similarly, 58% of 18-20 year olds were reconvicted within two years of a probation order compared to 71% of 16-17 year olds given a probation order and 79% of those aged 16 and under given a supervision order.

Previous criminal history

Studies have shown that the best predictor of future offending is past record. There is a clear relationship between number of previous court appearances and the likelihood of reoffending. Overall, about 60% of first court appearances given some form of community sentence or custody are reconvicted within two years. However, those with one or two previous convictions, 80% are reconvicted after a community sentence and 86% after custody. Among those with more than 7 previous court appearance, more than nine out of ten are reconvicted.

Local schemes

It is always possible that some local projects are more successful than others are. No information is available about the reconviction rates for programmes run by probation or social services departments locally. However, the Leicestershire junior attendance centre found that 92% of those who successfully completed the order were not reconvicted within two years.

Figure 2: **Proportion reconvicted of a standard list offence in two years. sample of 10-17 year olds convicted in 1994.**

Figure3: **Reconviction ratess by previous convictions. Sample of 10-17 year olds convicted in 1994.**

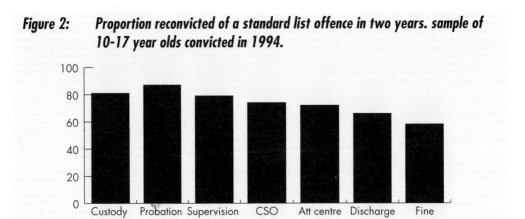

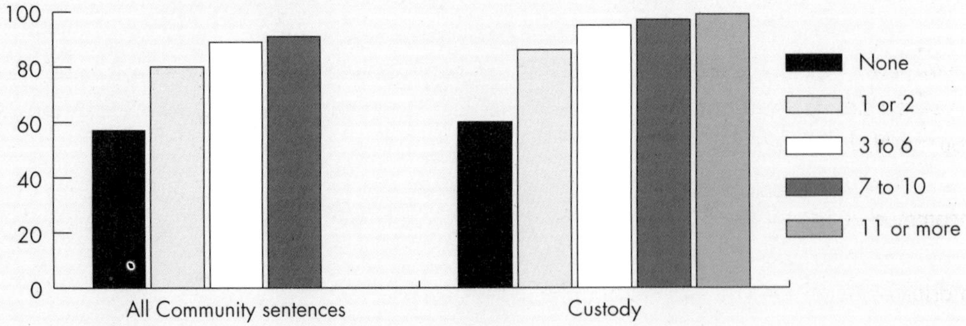

Appendix F

Court language

An important part of any attempt to engage defendants and parents in the court process is to use language that is clear and easily understandable. For those who work in courts on a daily basis it is easy to take much of the language of the court for granted; but for others it can be seen as 'jargon'. During the court observations a list of problematic words and phrases were recorded. These are phrases that were questioned by defendants or their parents, or unclear to observers. They are listed below in bold type and suggested alternative phrases are given alongside.

Community penalty – A sentence that you have to complete in the community.

Compliance – Go along with.

Concurrent – At the same time.

Consecutive – One after another.

Consolidate fines – Put all the fines that you have together into one sum.

Custody – Locked up (in a Young Offender Institution).

Date of birth – Birthday.

Do you have any means? – Are you receiving any money that you can use to pay a fine?

Dis-served – Not served.

If you fail to surrender then you render yourself liable to another offence of absconding – If you do not come back to court at the time that we have arranged this is an offence and you may be charged with it.

Incommoded – Unavailable.

In drink at the time – Drunk at the time.

Just received A.O. – You have just been given an attendance centre order.

Live witnesses – Witnesses who come to court to give evidence.

Lose your liberty – You may be locked up.

N.F.A. – No further action.

Peer group – Friends.

Prevaricate – Lie.

Remorse – Feel sorry.

Remit – The case will not be dealt with here – we will send it to 'X' court and they will deal with it from now on.

Retail premises – Shops.

Retire – We will leave the courtroom to consider what to do.

Stand down – This case will be put off for the moment, and we will call you back into court later.

The bench will… – The magistrates will…

The magistrates may decline jurisdiction today – The magistrates may decide that they cannot deal with the case today, as it is so serious that it will have to go to Crown Court.

We like juveniles to see the duty solicitor – We like people who appear at the Youth Court to see the 'duty solicitor', who is a solicitor here at the court that you can speak to for free.

Your licence will be endorsed – A record of these offences will be put on your driving licence.

You will be dealt with by the X bench – The magistrates in X will deal with this case

(To witness) You may be released – As you have given your evidence you may leave the courtroom.

References

Anderson, R. (1978). *Representation in the Juvenile Court*. London: Routledge and Kegan Paul.

Asquith, S. (1983). *Children and Justice: Decision Making in Children's Hearings and Juvenile Courts*. Edinburgh: Edinburgh University Press.

Crow, I. and Stubbing, T. (2000). 'Fast Tracking Persistent Young Offenders: to what effect?', *Liverpool Law Review*, 1-28.

Erickson, E. P. (1982). 'The Client's Perspective', in Martin, F. M. and Murray, K. (eds.). *The Scottish Juvenile Justice System*. Edinburgh: Scottish Academic Press.

Hedderman, C., Ellis, T. and Sugg, D. (1999). *Increasing confidence in community sentences: the results of two demonstration projects*. Home Office Research Study No. 194. London: Home Office.

Home Office. (1997). *'No More Excuses – a new approach to tackling youth crime in England and Wales'*, Cm 3809. London: The Stationery Office.

Home Office/Lord Chancellor's Department (1998). *Opening Up Youth Court Proceedings*.

Irvine of Lairg, Lord Chancellor (1998). *Improving Youth Justice*. Letter to the Chairmen of Youth Panels in England and Wales.

Mattinson, J. and Mirrlees-Black, C. (2000). *Attitudes to Crime and Criminal Justice: Findings from the 1998 British Crime Survey*. Home Office Research Study No. 200. London: Home Office.

Morris, A. and Giller, H. (1977). 'The Juvenile Court – The Client's Perspective'. *Criminal Law Review*, 198 – 205.

Parker, H., Casburn, M. and Turnbull, D. (1981). *Receiving Juvenile Justice: Adolescents and State Care and Control*. Oxford: Blackwell.

Plotnikoff, J. and Woolfson, R. (1998). *Witness Care in Magistrates' Courts and the Youth Court.* Research Findings No. 68. Home Office Research and Statistics Directorate. London: Home Office.

Scott, P. D. (1958), 'Juvenile Courts: The Juvenile's Point of View'. *British Journal of Delinquency,* 200 – 210.

Voelcker, P. M. W. (1960). 'Juvenile Courts: The Parent's Point of View'. *British Journal of Delinquency,* 154 – 166.

Notes

Notes

Notes

RDS Publications

Requests for Publications

Copies of our publications and a list of those currently available may be obtained from:

Home Office
Research, Development and Statistics Directorate
Communications Development Unit
Room 201, Home Office
50 Queen Anne's Gate
London SW1H 9AT
Telephone: 020 7273 2084 (answerphone outside of office hours)
Facsimile: 020 7222 0211
E-mail: publications.rds@homeoffice.gsi.gov.uk

alternatively

why not visit the RDS web-site at
          Internet: http://www.homeoffice.gov.uk/rds/index.htm

where many of our publications are availabe to be read on screen or downloaded for printing.